COAST  TZ

The Air Raids on Newhaven, Peacehaven and Seaford, during World War Two

David Rowland

This book is dedicated to the memory of my very good friend Harold 'H' Green, and his wife, Sheila. Harold was a member of the Brighton Police force and we had been friends for more than thirty years. Whilst I was researching and writing this book Harold and Sheila both passed away within a few weeks of each other.

By the same author:
Brighton Blitz, S.B.Publications, 1997

Published in 2001 by S.B.Publications
19 Grove Road
Seaford, East Sussex BN25 1TP

ISBN 185770 194 1

CONTENTS

Front Cover: Pelham Road, Seaford, after the raid on November 5, 1941.
                 The site is now occupied by Welbeck Court.
Back Cover: The electricity sub-station near Newhaven Town Station,
                 destroyed by bombs on September 10, 1940.

INTRODUCTION

Following the success of *Brighton Blitz* I was persuaded to write a follow-up, and this is it – the story of the war years on the coastal strip between Brighton and Seaford.

I had always imagined that Newhaven, being a port as well as a military town, would have suffered a larger number of air attacks than Seaford, but in reality it was Seaford that fared worse.

Once again, I have managed to find a number of people who were there and who have related their stories. During the air attack on November 5,1942, at Seaford, a fifteen-year-old girl, Betty Hamper, was trapped for more than six hours under the debris of a large building. I feel privileged to be able to tell a little of her marvellous, but sad story. There is also the tragic story of Folly Fields in Newhaven, where a number of people, several from the same family, lost their lives.

I continue to wonder why there are no monuments or memorials to those civilians who lost their lives through enemy action. Are they different from military personnel?

It never ceases to amaze me how kind and interested the general public are. I had a number of letters published in local newspapers requesting information, and each produced a good response. Many of those who wrote put me in touch with others, and the group grew and grew.

There are many people who deserve a mention for the great help they have given me. Don Lander, of Newhaven, contacted me in the very early part of my research and continued to do so right up to the end of it. His first-hand knowledge and information have been invaluable, giving a very human insight and making my job a lot easier.

I must also single out Mrs Connie King from Portslade who, like Don, wrote to me right at the beginning and furnished me with a lot of useful material.

One of the most interesting people I met whilst preparing this book was Bill Russell, from Peacehaven, who was an ARP warden in Newhaven during the war years. He saw, and took part in, many of the wartime incidents. Bob Truelove is to be thanked especially, for his knowledge and help in regard to his information about coastal defences.

Researching this type of book takes many hours poring over records, old newspapers and other documents, and I would like to thank the staff of East Sussex Record Office, Lewes, and in particular Jennifer Nash.

A number of people gave me invaluable help with the Betty Hamper story and these include Mrs Wilkie of Seaford, and Mrs Longhurst of Haywards

Heath. John Yates of Shoreham provided useful information about the rescue of his grandfather, Robert Cochrane, in Chichester Place, Brighton Generous help was also given by Peter Bailey, curator of Newhaven Museum, and the dedicated volunteers who man the museum.

I would also like to thank Pat Moorman, editor of *The Leader,* and staff members at the *The Argus*; Mrs S Stevens of Lewes District Council; Peter Holt from Eastbourne; Mr G Holliday from Seaford; Alan Parsons from Newhaven and Caralynne Ledingham for her computer skills.

Last, but not least, I must thank my wife Christine who once again has had to put up with me and a new book.

I hope I have not forgotten anyone who assisted, but should I have done so inadvertently, then I apologise for the oversight.

David Rowland

We shall go on to the end, we shall fight in France, we shall fight on the seas and oceans, we shall fight with growing confidence and growing strength in the air, we shall defend our island, whatever the cost may be, we shall fight on the beaches, we shall fight on the landing grounds, we shall fight in the fields and in the streets, we shall fight in the hills; we shall never surrender.

Winston Churchill
House of Commons
June 4, 1940

REFLECTIONS

Sitting comfortably in my favourite armchair one day, my thoughts drifted back to when I was a boy during the war years. These days I find it easier to remember those very exciting days than what I had for my last meal.

I lived in a row of working class terraced properties in Brighton, where front doors were rarely locked, except at night-time. I can recall one of our neighbours, Mrs Potiphar, walking through the front door, calling out 'Coo-ee', and my grandmother shouting out the same greeting, 'Coo-ee', as she clumped downstairs to greet her friend. Mrs Potiphar accepted the statutory cup of tea and then ran through the local gossip. I always half listened but paid far more attention if she started to talk about the latest bombings. Her gossip and cup of tea were both completed about the same time, as were the cigarettes that they both enjoyed. I knew when she was about to leave, as she would ask my grandmother if she could lend her a cup of sugar or a couple of slices of bread or even a spoonful of tea. She always paid it back. That was the way neigh-

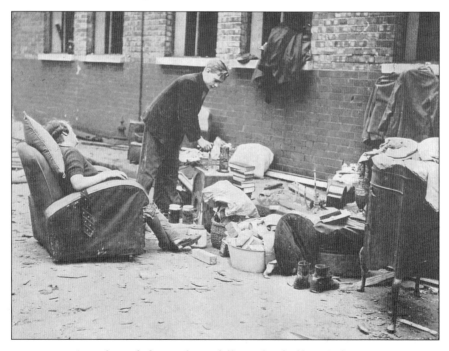

A much needed rest after a different kind of house cleaning

bours shared out their meagre rations. People then were leaner but fitter and possibly better nourished. I cannot recall seeing many fat people.

One of the most interesting and exciting places to play was in bombed houses. We children never fully realised just how dangerous these places were. My grandmother would tell me that I mustn't go anywhere near bombed houses, but to us, the more dangerous the building,

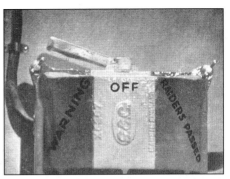

The air raid siren, first sounded at 11.42am on September 3, 1939

the more fun it was. Where there were several groups of children playing in these places, it was quite natural for each group to take one room and, within reason, stay in the confines of that room. However, the noise we made soon drew unwanted attention and it was usually not very long before we would be chased out either by one of the nearby residents or by the one person we all dreaded — the policeman. Although I had many close shaves, I never did get caught. I think it was after a friend fell through one of the ceilings to the floor below, breaking his arm, that we stopped going for a while.

At night time these smashed and broken houses showed up in the part light, making some very frightening shapes, very eerie, and there always seemed to be a whistling sound as the wind hurtled through. In one of the houses a man had been killed when a bomb struck and there was talk that he had come back – as a ghost. Adults used to say that they had seen him, and this served to make the area even more frightening to us. The bombed buildings were eventually demolished and a number of prefabricated homes replaced the terraced houses.

The once-a-year treat, at Christmas time, was a roast chicken dinner. Chicken was a very expensive scarce meat. Families like mine could not afford to buy it at any other time of the year. Some people bought a young cockerel and kept it in the backyard to fatten up for Christmas dinner. We had one and kept it in a large tea chest laid on its side, on house bricks. The open end was wired and had a small door for the bird to get out and wander around.

As the end of the year approached the chicken was not let out as it had to be plump for Christmas. I used to feed it but I didn't really appreciate what it was all about. I have a very vivid memory of the day, close to Christmas, when a neighbour was called in to kill the cockerel. He broke its neck but it ran around the garden for a few seconds with its head hanging down, before it fell to the ground. I was in floods of tears when I realised what had happened and made it quite clear that I wasn't going to eat it.

My grandmother told me that she had swapped ours for someone else's chicken, and duly prepared the bird for the table. It looked very appetising on a plate waiting and yes, I did eat it.

We used to have a lot of beef, which then was cheap. Most families followed a tried and tested weekly menu. For example on Sunday there would be roast beef, yorkshire pudding, potatoes and vegetables. On Monday it was cold roast beef with mashed potatoes. Sometimes, if there were any vegetables left over from Sunday's dinner, they would be fried into various types of 'bubble and squeak'.

On Tuesday there would still be a little bit of meat left, probably the fatty ends. Together with any meat bones from the Sunday joint, they would all go into a pot with any root vegetables available – potatoes, carrots, swede, turnips – and all would be stewed together for some hours. If there was not too much when it was dished out the meal would be supplemented by a thick slice of bread. There would be a meat pudding or pie on Wednesday and Thursday, and in our house, Friday's dinner was the one I really looked forward to. My Aunt Edie (who lived with us as her husband, Laurie, was a prisoner-of-war in Germany) would go off to the local fish and chip shop, (Pike's in Southover Street). Sometimes I would go with her. I always hated waiting in the long queue which would stretch quite a

long way up Southover Street. Fish and chips was always a very popular meal, mainly because it was so cheap.

In the summer holidays, armed with bread and jam sandwiches and a bottle of water, we children would walk out to Patcham to help the farmer at the top of Church Hill, I think his name was Dumbrell. Little did I know that more than fifty years later I would be writing about the B17 Flying Fortress that crash-landed in one of his fields.

Brighton schoolchildren learn to handle the smaller hoses of the stirrup pump

CURFEW ON THE SOUTH COAST

The curfew covered the area along the coast between Rottingdean and Seaford, including Newhaven. All civilians had to be indoors by 10pm, stated a compulsory Military Order issued on Thursday, July 4, 1940.

Public houses, places of amusement and cinemas were required to close their doors by that hour. No civilians or civilian vehicles were permitted to move about in the areas covered by the Order after 10pm. Anyone disobeying would be handed over by the military to the police.

Two areas were affected by the order. Area A took in Rottingdean, Newhaven and Tidemills in a line running from the Buckle Inn, Seaford, via the Sheffield Hotel, Newhaven, the Seaford Road railway arches, Gibbon Road, Newhaven (houses on either side were excluded), then northwards to the west side of Newhaven Infirmary, and on to the coast road to Rottingdean.

Area B covered Seaford south of a line from the west junction of Marine Drive and Claremont Road, Claremont Road and Church Street, Steyne Road and the junction of Steyne Road and Southdown Road, then east in a line running through the Seaford Head golf links, across the Cuckmere River to Exceat New Barn.

Military personnel and government employees, such as ARP wardens and Local Defence Volunteers, were allowed in the areas after 10pm on production of a pass.

Tanks at Rottingdean being greeted by villagers

THE BLACKOUT

Reading through the local newspapers while researching this book, I came across a number of court reports of blackout infringements. By law, everyone had to cover every window and door with a black material so that after dark no lights could be seen from the street. The object of this was to ensure that enemy aircraft had no light by which to guide their bombs

Air raid wardens and policemen patrolled the streets and should they see a chink of light they shouted 'put that blooming light out!' – words made familiar to a later generation through television's *Dad's Army*. That was the best that could happen to a culprit; the worst was to appear in court and have the case reported in the local newspaper. The punishment was usually a fine, but for persistent offences a prison sentence was possible. The police and the wardens were under strict orders to clamp down on those people guilty of showing a light as it could bring death and destruction on the locality.

The following report comes from the *Evening Argus* of July 26, 1940.

Mrs. Olivia Manning of 'Messellinia', Phyllis Avenue, Peacehaven, was summoned at Lewes Police Court on Tuesday, for permitting an unobscured light to be displayed from a roofed building at Peacehaven on July 12th, 1940.

P.C.Godley said that the light shone through French windows and lit up a 20 - foot conservatory. It was shining towards the sea.

The defendant, who wrote to the Court from London, asked the Bench to be lenient with her as it was her first offence. She was fined £3.

Another was:

At Lewes Police Court on Tuesday, 31st December, 1940. Mrs. Ethel Hollins of 'St.Martins', Roderick Avenue, Peacehaven was fined 10 shillings for an offence against the 'Black-out' regulations. P.C.Leggett gave evidence.

Shirts were worn outside trousers after dark so that the person in front could be seen in the blackout

These snippets from sixty years ago seem a little funny now, but they were viewed as very serious in war time.

BRIGHTON

As I mentioned in the Introduction, this book follows *Brighton Blitz*, published in 1997, a book that concentrated solely on the air attacks on Brighton during the Second World War. Since then further details have come to light of the raid on Tuesday, May 25, 1943, when twenty-four people were killed, and these I have included in this section. The story below, about the 'mummified hand', came to light quite unexpectedly while I was researching the times and dates of air raids in Seaford. These incidents, together with what I believe to be the first full list of air attacks on Brighton, will be included in an updated edition of *Brighton Blitz*.

THE MUMMIFIED HAND

It was Christmas, 1949. The war had been over for four years and everyone was looking forward to a festive season which promised to be the best for many a long year. Although quite a few items of food and clothing were still on ration or subject to certain restrictions, the people of Brighton were determined to enjoy the period.

Among them were the Rousseaus, Robert and Phyllis, a young couple who had recently set up home at 9 White Street, off Edward Street. The two bedroom house was opposite the scene of a terrible bombing during the evening of Wednesday, September 18, 1940, when the terraced houses received a direct hit that killed eleven people ranging in age from two nine-month-old girls to a couple aged seventy-eight and eighty-four.

One day when Phyllis was upstairs in her bedroom she thought she heard noises coming from the roof cavity, but as she could not immediately identify the sounds she put it down to her imagination. Then the noise came again, like a scratching sound, and Phyllis wondered if there were mice, or birds in the roof. She told Robert, who listened, heard nothing and dismissed it, believing that his twenty-three-year-old wife's imagination was running riot because she was pregnant.

Phyllis and Robert Rousseau
in the early 1950s

Devastation in White Street on the morning after the bomb

But the noises continued into January, heard only by Phyllis. When her brother George visited and she told him of the noises, both Robert and George decided to investigate to put Phyllis's mind at rest. They removed the trap hatch and Robert climbed in with his torch, shining it around the darkened space. Suddenly he gasped with shock and called for George to take a look at what he saw. The beam lit up a cobweb-covered human hand, wrist and fore-arm. The two men saw that it was a left hand, and had come from a woman. On the fourth finger was a gold signet ring in the shape of a snake. They saw, too, that the finger nails had obviously continued to grow after the hand was severed.

Further horror was to follow for, after the police were informed, and officers had climbed into the roof to see the gruesome exhibit, Robert was arrested and taken to the police station. He was interviewed at length, but later released without charge.

Enquiries were made to identify the hand, and publicity was given to the unusual snake ring. After some weeks a woman, living in Switzerland, con-tacted the police with information. After the bomb fell in 1940 two people were missing and never found. One was an airman, the other, a woman of fifty-two, the occupant of 6 White Street, who died together with her husband, Edward.

TUESDAY, MAY 25, 1943

Of all the air attacks on Brighton, three in particular stand out in people's memories. These three are always those that are most talked about when wartime is discussed.

Probably the best known was when the Odeon cinema, in St George's Road, Kemp Town, received a direct hit on Saturday, September 14, 1940. Forty-seven people were killed and a further 100 were injured. This day was certainly one that will remain paramount in the history of Brighton.

Another attack still talked about is known as 'the day they bombed the clinic'. This was on Monday, March 29, 1943. On this occasion sixteen people were killed and 121 injured.

The third was on Tuesday, May 25, 1943, when more than twenty-five Focke-Wulf 190s bombed and shot up the town. Within a few minutes on this day there were more than twenty separate bombing incidents. One happened in the eastern part of the town when a 500kg bomb fell on terraced houses in Chichester Place. It demolished numbers 17 and 19, and caused serious damage to adjoining houses. A number of people were buried beneath the rubble, including Robert Cochrane, who was seventy-nine years old. He lived at No.17 and it was a miracle that he was not killed when his home collapsed on top of him. Somehow he managed to stay alive until rescuers reached him twenty- three hours after the bomb exploded.

It needed many rescue units to work on this incident, and military units were brought in to help, a number of them being Canadian. Gradually, piece by piece, brick by brick, the debris was slowly moved away. Fortunately, because of double British summertime, daylight lasted well into the evening. Every so often the command 'Quiet!' would be heard, so that rescuers could listen for victims still alive.

As sunset – at 9.44pm that day – neared extra effort was put in; the rescuers knew that after dark the work would be slower. But as darkness fell the rescue went on, the men relentlessly moving everything that could be moved, with the aid of shaded lights. Even at the scene of a rescue it was imperative that naked lights were not shown so that enemy bombers could not use them as direction indicators.

All through the night the rescue continued. By daybreak the rescuers were close to exhaustion and fresh workers were brought in. They toiled throughout the morning and, soon after 11am, they at last made contact with Mr

Cochrane. He was injured, dirty and dishevelled, but alive.

Quickly but gently he was placed on a stretcher and was still able to raise a wry smile, despite his injuries, as he was put into an ambulance and taken to the Royal Sussex County Hospital. There the staff who treated him all said how impressed they were by his fighting spirit. Initially he responded to treatment, but early the following morning his health deteriorated and he died soon after 10am.

Robert Cochrane

Robert Cochrane had lived in Chichester Place with his wife, Sarah, who was out shopping with their daughter Dora when the bomb fell. He was a popular figure in Kemp Town and was often seen walking along the sea front. He was born in Edinburgh in 1864 and worked as a blacksmith-engineer on the railway until his retirement at sixty five, after which he continued with the rail company as a night watchman.

The following is an excerpt from Sarah Cochrane's diary, dated Tuesday, May 25, 1943:

> Went to Dora's 12 o' clock noon. At 20 past 12 a terrible raid, Air, which completely wiped out my home, burying poor Dad, Mrs. Walder, a dear

The rescue scene at 17 and 19 Chichester Place

14

little woman, and Chum, Chrissie's Dog. Mrs. Walder killed outright and Chum but poor Dad buried for 24 hours, what a dreadful night. Soldiers and Sailors working like slaves digging to find him, located him in the early hours of Wednesday morning, alive. Yes, by God's good grace alive. What a dreadful ordeal for him, pinned down by the shoulders for 24 hours; brought up gently into the open air, amidst the hushed crowd of hundreds of people. Doctors and Nurses waiting to care for him, God bless them all; taken to hospital. Went to see him in the afternoon. Poor Dad recognised me at once, we kissed each other, and all the past was forgiven. Asked me if I had been to the pictures; I had been so long away he thought, not really realising he was in hospital, to me he seemed very ill, and I had no hope he would live, saw him again with Georgie. "Hello, my son" he said, "anything the matter". "No Dad" Georgie said; "only come to see you". He knew everyone, so we left him with a kiss from all of us. He passed away soon after into God's safe keeping fully pardoned through the Cross of our Dear Saviour. Rest in Peace, dear, one day I hope I too will lie beside you, in that lovely spot, where the Sea breezes from our dear Sailor son's grave will pass over us both, and our spirits will be with him and our other dear babies above. To our other dear children who will often come to our last resting place God Bless and keep you all in his safe keeping. Do not fret or weep for us, but sing: We'll meet again tomorrow, Hope will banish sorrow. In all things trust in our Lord and Saviour, Jesus Christ, who to me is very real indeed and never forgets to answer our Prayers. Not in our way, but in His own loving way, for He knows our real needs more than we do ourselves. So trust Him even unto the End.

PEACEHAVEN and TELSCOMBE

MONDAY, SEPTEMBER 9, 1940

Telscombe residents heard the wail of the sirens at about 10.43pm on this day, indicating their first air attack.

A single aircraft, possibly a Junkers Ju 88, was spotted in the darkness some 100 yards offshore at Saltdean, flying eastwards. Shore batteries opened up but failed to hit the aircraft. It gained height and released three high explosive bombs that detonated on the beach and cliff edge about fifty yards east of where the Badgers Watch pub now stands.

Slight damage – a door blown off and windows broken – was caused to a couple of cliff top dwellings.

On this same night, London suffered several air attacks. Enemy aircraft suffered a number of casualties, including fifty two destroyed, eleven probably destroyed and another thirteen damaged.

It is possible that this aircraft's mission was also to bomb London, but for reasons unknown the pilot turned to a softer target.

SATURDAY, SEPTEMBER 21, 1940

A few minutes after 5pm on Saturday, September 21, 1940, a single raider dropped three smallish bombs on Downland, just north of Rodmell Avenue, Saltdean. One house sustained roof damage, broken windows and a cracked ceiling and a second had its windows broken. Nobody was injured.

SUNDAY, OCTOBER 6, 1940

At 12.20pm on Sunday, October 6, 1940 a single aircraft was spotted over the Channel, possibly three miles out from Peacehaven, flying west to east. It was suggested later that the aircraft was probably hunting for coastal shipping.

It may be that the crew became bored as the aircraft turned in over the Peacehaven coastline and released three high explosive bombs. One fell in Tor Road, striking a bungalow called Littlewood Lodge, which was considerably damaged, while the occupant was slightly injured. A second bomb demolished and set fire to Rose Cottage in Glynn Road. Fortunately it was unoccupied at the time. Three other properties received blast damage, and another two received slight damage, with just broken windows.

Rescue services were soon on the scene, taking care of the casualty and extinguishing the fire.

The remains of Rose Cottage in Glynn Road

SATURDAY, NOVEMBER 2, 1940

It was 7.15am on a very cold morning, and many people were still in their beds. Suddenly, two German aircraft came in low, flying south east to north west. They were accompanied by the sirens, the pips (warning that the enemy was directly overhead) and anti-aircraft gunfire.

The raiders dropped seventeen small high explosive bombs in a concentrated arc, striking a number of residential properties. They quickly crossed the Tye, turned and sped back across the Channel.

The first two bombs exploded on the foreshore, and although they made a very loud noise, there was no damage. The next one struck the cliff top, some yards west of the area now known as The Esplanade, and another struck the main coast road. None of these bombs caused any significant damage.

The next few bombs fell in and around residential properties. One fell just east of the Union Church, causing some damage to the church windows and very slight blast damage. Yet another exploded in the garden of a house close by. This caused slight damage to the rear of the property.

The seventh bomb landed close to the junctions of Amhurst and Buckhurst Roads and then failed to explode. People were evacuated from the area and a UXB (unexploded bomb) sign was installed. The bomb went off a few hours later, again causing minimal damage.

The next bomb scored a direct hit on a residential property called Bubzone in Tyedean Road. This caused considerable damage as did another which

17

exploded seconds later on the east side of Tyedean Road. Two other bombs struck the opposite side of the road causing considerable blast damage to several houses.

The eleventh bomb struck a house called Garth, in Springfield Avenue, causing damage to the cesspit – an event that prompted a few lighthearted laughs and jokes. Another bomb also landed in Springfield Road, severely damaging a house called Raycot, where the occupant was injured. This was the only injury, from this raid, that required hospital treatment. A small fire broke out but it was soon brought under control.

The thirteenth bomb struck yet another house in Springfield Avenue, called Sunningdale, causing roof damage, a split door and broken windows.

The final three bombs fell and exploded in a field just to the north of Springfield Avenue, causing slight damage to four houses.

The Civil Defence and rescue workers were quickly on the scene, assisting the occupants to clear up the debris, and the first aid team attended to three residents who suffered slight injuries but needed no further treatment.

FRIDAY, NOVEMBER 15, 1940

The Butlins building in Longridge Avenue was taken over by the National Fire Service (NFS) as a training centre for the duration. On a number of occasions towards the end of the London Blitz, there were exchanges of firemen between London and other areas, and the South Coast.

This had been a very wet evening and night, with a large number of heavy showers. Sunset was at 5.09pm, but it was dark a while before then. It was the day after the infamous Coventry attack, when very serious damage was inflicted on that city.

At 12.03am the sound of an enemy aircraft was heard, gradually getting louder, and warnings were given. People took shelter, expecting to hear explosions at any moment, but everything was strangely quiet, and the sound of aircraft engines could no longer be heard.

What the residents did not know was that between thirty and forty incendiary bombs had been dropped. Two landed on a house called St Michaels in Homebush Avenue, East Saltdean, causing a small fire in the roof area. The residents, assisted by the neighbours did what they could, but were powerless to stop serious damage being caused.

Another thirty or so incendiary bombs were dropped across a wide area on Telscombe Tye, causing no damage. One fell on the cliff top, just south of Longridge Avenue, but failed to go off.

FRIDAY, NOVEMBER 22, 1940

At 1.27pm on this dry, cold but cloudy day, the warning sirens indicated the approach of enemy aircraft. As people took shelter, a German aircraft, almost certainly a Dornier Do17, was seen approaching the coastline at low altitude. Suddenly, it turned away to the west and then released its bomb load of twelve small high explosive bombs – which dropped harmlessly into the sea and exploded.

This caused a staccato of explosions, sending a huge cascade of water some 50ft high about a quarter of a mile south of the Portobello outfall.

At about this time word was circulating that a German bomber had been shot down near Newhaven, and the crew killed. Was this the reason why the Do17 suddenly turned tail and dropped its bomb load?

THURSDAY, MARCH 13, 1941

The sirens sounded at 9.33pm on this Thursday evening, warning of an impending attack. Residents just had time to take cover in their shelters when a German bomber, possibly a Dornier Do17, approached the coastline from the east and dropped a number of small bombs.

One high explosive bomb fell in Cissbury Avenue, causing blast damage to three properties, and two incendiary bombs fell on Merryweather, starting a fire which destroyed the house. The two occupants were slightly injured.

Two other high explosive bombs fell in Southview Road, causing slight damage to four properties. Yet another bomb fell in Firle Road but failed to explode, and people in the area were hastily evacuated.

A number of incendiaries, estimated at 140, were dropped as well as the high explosive bombs. These all fell in the residential area. Many small fires occurred as a result but were quickly put out by the residents, aided by the Civil Defence workers. The two people who were injured were treated at the scene and did not attend hospital.

The UXB exploded at 12.50am the next day, causing some minor damage to properties in the vicinity.

TUESDAY, APRIL 8, 1941

The night was cloudy with moderate visibility. At about 11.30pm residents were awakened by the warning sounds as an enemy aircraft approached from the sea. A single aircraft dropped in the region of 150 incendiary bombs, these being scattered over Telscombe Tye, with a number falling at the southern end, close to Portobello. The only damage was a rather spectacular fire as a large patch of gorse bushes burned. The NFS soon had the problem under control. There was no damage caused to property. One fireman suffered a small injury – a burn to the left hand.

WEDNESDAY, APRIL 9, 1941

People had just returned to bed from the incendiary raid less than two hours earlier, when they were once more seeking shelter. Again it was a lone air-craft, almost certainly a Messerschmitt ME109. This one, flying close to the coastline, dropped a single high explosive bomb that exploded at the south end of the Tye, close to the roadway. A number of properties suffered roof damage, broken windows and minor blast damage. There was no report of injuries.

MONDAY, OCTOBER 21, 1941

There is very little detail on this particular air-attack. The records state only that a single aircraft dropped one incendiary bomb at 9.40pm and this caused a minor fire to the roof of a house in Central Avenue. The fire was quickly put out by neighbours with the aid of a stirrup pump.

SUNDAY, NOVEMBER 5, 1944

The only details on this air attack are that one high explosive bomb fell on the south east area of Telscombe Tye, causing slight damage to four properties. No injuries were recorded.

NOTES FROM THE WAR RECORDS

At about 9.30am on Tuesday, February 18, 1941, PC Fred Leggett went from Peacehaven Police Station to The Warren, a large property in Telscombe Cliffs Way. He was met by Captain James Mackay and a large stray barrage balloon. The balloon cable had become entangled in the Captain's 60ft flag staff, and this had snapped off about 4ft from the base. The long section of the staff was wedged in a pine tree, thus anchoring the balloon.

The cable had also become entangled in the stable roofing dislodging a num-ber of tiles and had fused the lighting system. RAF Tangmere was informed and the balloon was later removed by airmen from RAF Tichfield.

At about 7.30am on Monday, March 15, 1942, a naval barrage balloon was found in Horsham Avenue. It was initially guarded by the local police and later collected by naval personnel from Newhaven.

On Tuesday, October 5, 1942, a stray barrage balloon was located at Hoddern Farm, Peacehaven. The RAF at Newhaven Harbour was informed and later attended, collecting the balloon.

NEWHAVEN

ALTHOUGH a port town, and one used by the military, Newhaven saw relatively little activity from the enemy, suffering only forty-one incidents between 1939 and 1945.

The official statistics show that during the whole length of the war there were 1,057 local air raid alerts, many of which were false. There is some difficulty in establishing the exact number of air attacks as many of the records are missing. The twenty-seven known raids recorded here do not include attacks on nearby villages.

Air attacks were responsible for the deaths of fifteen members of the civilian population with another forty-seven suffering varying degrees of injuries. Eleven of the fifteen dead were killed in just one incident and by just one bomb. This was at Folly Fields, on Wednesday, December 11, 1940, a night that Newhaven should never forget.

The records show that thirteen properties were completely destroyed, forty others were severely damaged but were able to be repaired, and 540 were slightly damaged as a result of enemy action. But this cannot compare with the damage caused when, on November 22, 1944, a barge broke away from its tug, struck a mine and the cargo of 180 tons of high explosives went up. It

The Newhaven schoolboys who were evacuated to Thurleigh, Bedfordshire, in 1940, pictured with schoolmaster Mr Gilson

was fortunate for Newhaven that the barge had drifted below the cliffs, which masked a lot of the explosion that followed. This one incident caused three times more damage than the enemy inflicted during six years of war.

Newhaven harbour was under Navy control with the Army moving in along the coastline. Anti-aircraft guns were set up around Bishopstone and Denton. Installations for fuelling Navy vessels were set up along the beach, just west of Tidemills.

An ex-London, Brighton and South Coast Railway 10-ton wagon was pushed along to the Buckle end of the line. It contained a concrete casement with firing slits, just like the battlements of a castle.

Also in this vicinity was an apparatus for setting the sea on fire, placed there in preparation for a possible German invasion. Anti-tank traps and dannert wire were also laid along the length of the beach.

The Local Defence Volunteers (LDV) unit had been formed in June 1940, soon after to be renamed the Home Guard. In Newhaven, railwaymen volunteers were formed into the 2nd Battalion Southern Railway Home Guard. They were trained by the Duke of Cornwall's Light Infantry, and had a reputation as a much more formidable force than the average Dad's Army. Throughout the war, staff regularly patrolled the railway lines at night.

Inside the underground Naval control centre at South Heighton

23

WEDNESDAY, JULY 3, 1940

The first recorded attack on Newhaven was on this Wednesday when a single aircraft approached from the south west at 9.20am. The first target for its machine guns was a group of soldiers spread along the beach. They had already dived for cover on hearing the approach of the aircraft. It then turned to the town and used its machine guns as it passed over. The sirens had sounded as the aircraft approached the coast and people had already taken to the shelters and any other cover they could find.

The machine- gunning of the town caused some minor damage – a few broken windows and roof tiles – but there had been no casualties. Just when everyone thought that the trouble had passed, the aircraft returned, obviously bound for its base across the Channel. This time it came in lower and once again strafed the town.

The local guns opened up as it reached the southern part of the harbour, where it dropped its payload of bombs. There were six, all of which landed in the sea just outside the harbour.

The possible target was the inspection ship HMS *Schievan,* which was not damaged. There were no recorded casualties.

THE SAME DAY

The time was 5.37pm as the steam train pulled out of Seaford Station on its

*The ex-steam yacht Schievan was stationed at the harbour
approaches to check passing vessels*

Locomotive engine 2244, which bore its scars until scrapped in 1949

way to Horsted Keynes. The train was a D1 tank engine, No 2244 and was the 'push and pull' type, that is the engine was pushing from the rear. The driver was Charles Pattenden, aged fifty-nine, who lived in Eridge Road, Tunbridge Wells, and had been a train driver for many years. His guard was a Mr E Batchelor.

There were not many passengers on board as the train trundled along towards Newhaven. It was right on time as it passed through Bishopstone Beach Halt, and it was about this time that a single German bomber was seen fast approaching the coast. As the train left the halt for the exposed Tidemills stretch of the line, the enemy opened fire on it.

There was little the passengers could do but crouch on the carriage floor.

The aircraft then delivered its load of six bombs, which exploded at Oyster Ponds, not far from the halt. The train had by this time come to a halt and, although it was not struck, it felt the force and suffered blast damage. A splinter struck the driver, causing severe injury, and he died a short time later. The guard was also struck and received a serious back injury.

One of the passengers, Mrs P Steward, of Brighton Road, Newhaven, and a friend, saw the plane swoop down and heard two explosions. The force of the attack blew the toe off Mrs Steward's right shoe. The windows were smashed and the carriage filled with fragments of flying glass.

Also on the train were two women, Mrs Terrell of Lawes Avenue, Newhaven, and Mrs Matthews of Paddock Road, Lewes, and Mrs Terrell's two children, a daughter of four and a son, Ronald, who was one year old. Mrs Terrell said: 'It happened so quickly. All the windows were smashed and

25

we had lots of splinters of glass in our hair. My son had a cut near one eye and the back of my coat was marked, as if it had been scorched.'

> **Charles Henry Pattenden, 59, of 37 Eridge Road, Tunbridge Wells**

THURSDAY, AUGUST 22, 1940

At 10.50pm the sirens started to wail and people in the town made their way to the air raid shelters. They had had their first taste of bombing the previous month, but that was in the daytime. This was at night and, somehow, it seemed worse. Soon the sound of an aircraft was heard and the townsfolk braced themselves for what might happen.

The single aircraft dropped four incendiary bombs on houses in Brighton Road, just at the junction with Lewes Road. Small fires were started in the roofs of two adjoining properties, but they were quickly extinguished by the residents and helpful neighbours. There were no injuries.

MONDAY, SEPTEMBER 9, 1940

On what was described as 'a quiet and pleasant evening' those people who had been out for a stroll before going to bed were suddenly forced to run, seeking shelter as the sirens signalled danger at about 9.39pm. The pips followed just as the sound of an incoming plane was heard.

The enemy came in from the south west. It flew over the town, machine gunning the streets. This caused very little damage and no injuries. The plane then made a return pass, and above the harbour it dropped three bombs, which landed within a few yards of each other on grassland some 600 yards to the east of the Harbour Station. The bombs made sizeable craters and were estimated to have been the largest dropped on Newhaven so far. Possibly they were of 50kg.

TUESDAY, SEPTEMBER 10, 1940

At tea time a single aircraft approached the coast at a fairly high level, flying straight over the town before the sirens had given their warning. People were standing in the High Street pointing up at the plane which, at that stage, posed no threat.

But when it banked to the left and started back towards the town, those in the High Street were soon diving for cover. The aircraft lost some of its altitude,

The electricity sub-station near Town Station, Newhaven,
destroyed by bombs on September 10, 1940

and appeared to be searching for a target. It dropped two high explosive bombs that struck the electricity sub-station near to the Town Station next to the railway tracks. The sub-station was demolished and a number of yards of railway track were damaged. Damage was also caused to nearby rolling stock.

A number of windows in nearby properties were blown out by the blast but, remarkably, there were no serious injuries.

The aircraft very quickly gained height and flew off in a south-easterly direction, escaping the fire of the harbour guns.

THURSDAY, SEPTEMBER 12, 1940

It was just after 4pm when the sirens started to wail and people quickly made for the shelters. Once again the town came under machine-gun attack, and again there were no injuries. The single aircraft circled the town twice and then flew almost directly southwards along the length of the harbour.

The harbour defences gave a good account of themselves but whether the aircraft was hit is unknown. It dropped a single bomb at the harbour mouth near to what the newspaper described as an examination vessel, possibly the *Schievan*.

THURSDAY, SEPTEMBER 26, 1940

On this day the sirens and the pips were sounded at the same time, at 4.50pm, when a number of German aircraft were seen approaching from the south west. Locals were not to know that they were about to witness their worst air attack of the war so far.

The Catholic church after the raid

It appears to have been part of a concerted attack right along the south coast from Dover to Southampton – where thirty-six people were killed and sixty injured. Eastbourne also suffered badly in the same raid.

Newhaven was attacked by a number of aircraft identified as Messerschmitt Bf110s and possibly Bf109s. Between them they dropped nineteen high explosive bombs in various parts of the town. The planes also opened up with cannon fire. The only injury was caused to a naval rating who was on the river in a small boat.

One bomb demolished the front of the Roman Catholic church in Fort Road. A number of houses were demolished and many suffered serious damage. The worst hit areas were Meeching Court Farm, Gibbon Road, Hillcrest Road, Fort Road and the harbour area. The raid lasted less than three minutes.

THURSDAY, OCTOBER 10, 1940

Five minutes before 11pm the sirens and pips indicated another attack from the air – but no aircraft were heard. A bomber, possibly a Junkers 88, crossed the coast at Peacehaven and as it approached the golf course on the Brighton

Road its engines were switched off and the plane glided across the town. It dropped seven bombs. The first struck 7 and 9 Brighton Road, causing extensive damage. Another scored a direct hit on 1 Saxon Road, demolishing it and causing extensive damage to number 3. Fortunately the family from number 1 was away at the time.

An unusual feature of this raid was that one bomb exploded in mid-air, over Lewes Road. This caused considerable damage in the area to windows and roofs, and nine people were hurt, mainly from flying glass. Rescue and first aid teams treated eight of the injured, and the ninth was taken to hospital.

The most serious incident was at the convent on Church Hill. Here, three bombs fell, killing one of the nuns and damaging the building severely. Rescue work went on for much of the night by the light of shaded lamps, which made progress slow, dangerous and very difficult. Several of the nuns were buried in the debris, but only three needed hospital treatment. The nun who died was French-born Louise Mauger, a Sister of Mercy.

Yet another bomb landed in the garden of 7 Saxon Road. Don Lander, who lived there, said he was in bed and just about to go off to sleep when he heard bombs whistling down. 'One, which I believed had my name on it, fell just fifteen feet from where I lay in bed, but fortunately didn't go off,' he said. 'We were turned out in a hurry and went to stay with friends. I can recall another bomb demolishing 1 Saxon Road and half of number 3.'

Bill Russell, a Civil Defence worker in Newhaven during the war years, was living at 30 Brighton Road with his wife and a girl lodger at the time of this raid. He said: 'The night the convent was bombed, I recall that for some reason we didn't go to the shelter. We had an Anderson shelter in the rear garden. We were sleeping in the front of the house and the girl at the back. Without any warning, bombs started falling. At this time the sirens hadn't sounded. I remember that we

The former convent pictured in 1998

30 Brighton Road, Newhaven

got out of bed in a hurry, wondering quite what was going on. I then saw that our garden was lit up, just as though it were the fifth of November. It was quite an incredible sight. What happened was that an oil bomb had landed in our back garden. A piece of shrapnel crashed through the window and landed right on the pillow. This was where our young girl lodger had been sleeping (the girl was shocked, but unhurt).'

'Meanwhile, another bomb had fallen on the opposite side of the road to us. It was a small one but it demolished the house. We considered ourselves very lucky as our house suffered only minor damage.'

'When the sirens sounded it was a signal to me to report for duty and so I set out to get my vehicle. The vehicle we used was an old soft top charabanc. The seats had been ripped out in order that we could load up our tools. I made my way up to Church Hill, where I had been sent. When I arrived the place was an absolute mess. There was chaos and confusion. A number of rescue workers had already arrived. I recall that there were a couple of people asking for some assistance, while a few others just sat on a small piece of concrete – shocked. There was only one death, a nun, and there was nothing we could do for her. She was lying in bed with a large beam right across the upper part of her body. I think she had been killed outright. It was very sad.'

'We set about our work, but it was rather dangerous as one of the walls was very unsafe. It was pretty obvious that we would have to bring the wall down. A steel hawser was fitted around the wall and the other end was attached to the front of my vehicle. I reversed it and the wall came crashing down in a great cloud of dust and dirt. We continued to work on, completely unaware that close to where we had been for most of the night, was an unexploded bomb.'

Louise Mauger, 52, Sister of Mercy, a French citizen

MONDAY, OCTOBER 14, 1940

During the evening, at about 7.45pm, a single German aircraft appeared from north of Seaford, travelling westwards. A witness said it looked like a Messerschmitt. The enemy aircraft dropped a couple of bombs and sped off over the Channel. The two bombs, one a high explosive and the other an oil bomb, were dropped near Ledbury House, Seaford Road, Denton. No damage or injuries were reported, but a cow was injured and had to be destroyed.

THE SAME DAY

Later that evening two Messerschmitt Bf109s, each carrying two bombs, crossed the coastline west of Newhaven. Their target appears to have been the Fort. The four bombs were dropped and exploded on the cliffs close to the Fort but no damage was reported. The local defences opened up but no damage was inflicted on the fleeing aircraft.

MONDAY, OCTOBER 28, 1940

It had just turned 5pm and people were on their way home from work and from shopping when the sirens began to wail, with the pip sounds close behind, indicating the close proximity of German aircraft. The townsfolk were still making their way to shelters as fifteen or more Messerschmitt 109s appeared over Newhaven.

They passed several times over the town, their crews machine-gunning indiscriminately. Then the bombs came raining down, exploding with great ferocity and noise. One hit 56 South Road, seriously injuring Mary Bollen, eleven, who was in the Anderson shelter. Although the emergency services reached her quickly they were unable to save the child, and she died half an hour after

Newhaven Baptist Church

31

the bomb struck the house. The same bomb also injured seven others in the shelter; three were very badly hurt and were taken to hospital.

Another bomb struck a house in Meeching Avenue, injuring five people, and a bomb on Western Road caused minor injuries to two more.

Thirty other bombs were dropped that night, striking the Fort, the harbour and nearby streets, resulting in another six people being injured, two of whom needed hospital treatment. An oil bomb was also dropped but the location was not recorded.

The Baptist church lost its beautiful windows, while the roof of the Congregational Church School suffered severe damage.

The *Sussex Express* reported:

> Despite the intensity of the raid, the inhabitants of the town stood their ordeal in splendid fashion. The Civil Defence Services performed their work in a manner that won praise from all quarters, while the general public displayed to the full the grim and gay spirit of the times.

Mary Bollen, 11, 56 South Road, Newhaven

FRIDAY, NOVEMBER 1, 1940

At 7.20pm on this, All Hallowes day, an incoming aircraft, believed to be a Messerschmitt Bf109, machine-gunned the town as it passed over. It then dropped one small high explosive bomb on farm land at Meeching Court Farm. The raid lasted little more than thirty seconds, and there were no injuries or damage reported.

THE SAME DAY

At 8.45pm the sirens again heralded the approach of a German aircraft, possibly a Junkers 88. As seemed the case on almost every air attack, the aircraft first circled Newhaven and then, after machine-gunning the town, dropped its bombs.

These bombs, four in total, landed in the vicinity of Drove Road. Three hit the roadway, exploding immediately, and fracturing gas and water mains. The fourth, believed to be an oil bomb, landed on marshy ground nearby. Telephone wires were brought crashing to the ground. The loss of these three services was felt for a couple of days until repairs were effected.

SUNDAY, NOVEMBER 17, 1940

This attack started at about 3.50pm on a rather wet and cold Sunday afternoon when most people were staying by their firesides. Following raids on shipping in the Channel, and on targets in Kent, a sweep of German fighters, almost certainly Messerschmitt Bf109s, turned their attention to Newhaven. An eye witness saw them coming in from the north east – fast and low, and in just two minutes they wreaked havoc on the town.

The official records show that eight high explosive bombs were dropped. The first two fell in Wellington Road, Denton, causing some considerable damage to two houses and two others in the immediate vicinity were classed as seriously damaged. This resulted in seven people suffering injuries, three being serious, and they were quickly rushed to hospital.

Another bomb fell and exploded in Wheatley's yard, in The Drove. Two people here were slightly injured and received first aid treatment from local rescue workers.

Five bombs were dropped in the brooks to the south of Drove Road, and as they exploded they set off a great number of land mines. Considerable damage was caused to properties in Railway Road. There was also a bomb blast at the power station which littered the roads with the smashed glass of hundreds of windows.

Many properties nearby – in Railway Approach, High Street, Bridge Street and Chapel Street, suffered considerable damage to windows and roofs. Two other people were injured and were treated in hospital.

SUNDAY, DECEMBER 8, 1940

It had been a dark, wet and dismal day. The clouds were low and the wind, from the west, had blown fiercely for most of the day. It was not weather for an air raid. Sunset was not for another half an hour, yet it was already dark when, suddenly and without warning, the distinctive sound of an enemy aircraft was heard. The defence services went on immediate alert as the sirens started their wail. 'It wasn't much of a raid, four bombs were dropped, and the plane had gone,' said witness Bill Epsen. 'It was so quick that I didn't see anything. I heard the bombs go off, they were quite loud but sort of muffled.'

The official report states that a single aircraft dropped four high explosive bombs. Three landed at the brooks north of the concrete bridge, and the only damage was to the windows and roofs of nearby properties. The fourth bomb landed in the sea close to the East Pier, causing no damage. The aircraft then made off across the Channel.

MONDAY, DECEMBER 9, 1940

At 5.30am on a very dark and dismal morning, just a few hours after the previous day's raid, the sirens were wailing again, but there was more than enough time to reach shelter as nothing happened immediately. Some people started to leave their shelters, thinking that it was a false alarm, but they soon hurried back as an enemy aircraft was heard approaching and local guns started firing as the plane circled the town, machine-gunning before dropping one bomb.

It landed and exploded on the cliff top, approximately 300 yards south of St Ediths, Harbour Heights. This caused no injuries and only slight damage to some homes and other properties.

WEDNESDAY, DECEMBER 11, 1940

At 11.35pm this day Newhaven suffered its worst attack of the war years. The night was dark, with no moon showing. It had been raining and the roads were wet. There was a distinct chill in the air as winter approached.

Newhaven ARP members at Court Farm, Fort Road (now Meeching Court flats).
SE Rivett, chief warden, is fourth from the left. With him are A Wiltshire,
K Wheeler, J Whitbread, D Davis, Bert Russell and Mrs Nash.

The Luftwaffe had sent over almost 300 bombers with fighter escort, their main target being Birmingham. However, a number of aircraft carried out attacks on other targets, including southern England.

Seven aircraft attacked Brighton that night and perhaps one of these went on to bomb Newhaven. Although the attack on Brighton was seen as 'lucky' as the four 500kg bombs dropped failed to explode, the one 500kg bomb that fell on Newhaven killed and injured many.

The bomb scored a direct hit on three homes in Folly Field, Lewes Road, completely demolishing one and causing very serious damage to the other two. Thomas John Tapp of 7 Folly Field was flung from his bed into the street by the force of the explosion. He was found by rescuers a few minutes later, in his pyjamas, wandering in the street in a dazed state, unable to understand what had happened. Suddenly it dawned upon him that his wife and children were buried under the debris. He left the rescue team and ran back to the ruins of his home, screaming and tearing away at the debris with his bare hands. He was shouting out the names of his wife and children as he moved brick after brick. The wreckage was mountainously high and it was some hours before rescuers could reach the buried people. Mr Tapp was comforted

All that was left of the three houses in Folly Field

and eventually allowed himself to be led away, but he would not move far from the dreadful scene. He was not to know, then, that his wife and baby daughter had been killed.

Within a few minutes of the bomb exploding most of the rescue services were at the scene and the job was quickly under way. Shortly afterwards a number of military personnel arrived to help.

The scene was strangely quiet, only the noise of the debris being moved was heard. Rescuers knew that there were children buried under the rubble and they worked quickly, but carefully. Soon they heard the pitiful cries of young children – two distinct voices. A cry for 'quiet' went up and again the young voices were heard.

The team concentrated their efforts but, after an hour, the cries of one of the children ceased, and the rescuers became desperate. About three hours after the massive bomb had torn the little terrace apart, a young girl was reached and pulled from the debris. She was cold, very frightened but, miraculously, only slightly injured. She was still clutching the hand of her dead sister.

The five Tucknotts, who lived at 9 Folly Fields, all perished. They were Florence, forty, Herbert, forty-two and their children Hazel, eighteen, Herbert, sixteen and Doris, six. When the family was reached, only young Herbert was still alive, but he died of his injuries on December 16 in the Royal Sussex County Hospital. Hazel was on the doorstep, saying goodnight to her boyfriend, Frank Bartlett, when the bomb fell. Frank, also eighteen, who died with his sweetheart, had lived with his mother in Lower Place. During that terrible night Hazel's body was found in the debris, but there was no sign of Frank. In the early hours of the following morning, soon after it was light, someone in Folly Field was looking out towards the river and noticed that one of the houses in Lower Place, where Frank lived, had a hole in the roof. Rescue workers investigated and found the body of Frank Bartlett in the loft space of 16 Lower Place, next door to his own home.

Property up to half a mile from the explosion was damaged.

Bill Russell, a member of Newhaven Civil Defence, was one of the rescuers. This was the incident he remembered above all others. He said: 'It was a terrible night, all those people killed. When I first arrived on the scene I just could not believe what I saw. The place was just a pile of rubble – a very big pile. One man jumped out of a window and into the street as the bomb exploded. His family, sadly, were under the pile of rubble.

'The bomb struck the top house of the terrace, it then took on a domino effect, as the other houses just collapsed against each other going down hill. In what seemed a short while there were many people working at the site. Apart from us there were the police and, I think, army and navy personnel. We all pitched in together. We all knew it was a massive task facing us.'

Folly Field as it appears today – part of Newhaven's ring road.

> **Frank Bartlett, 18, 18 Lower Place, Newhaven**
> **Albert Victor Dartnell, 54, ARP warden, 8 Folly Field**
> **Mary Ann Dartnell, 74, 8 Folly Field**
> **Joan Reed, 29, 7 Folly Field**
> **Leonard Reed, 13 months, 7 Folly Field**
> **Alice Edith Tapp, 27, 49 Gibbon Road, Newhaven, at 7 Folly Field**
> **June Tapp, 2, 49 Gibbon Road, Newhaven, at 7 Folly Field**
> **Doris Tucknott, 6, 9 Folly Field**
> **Florence Tucknott, 40, 9 Folly Field**
> **Hazel Tucknott, 18, 9 Folly Field**
> **Herbert John Tucknott, 42, 9 Folly Field**
> **Herbert William Tucknott, 16, 9 Folly Field**

The *Sussex Express* reported that the funerals of all the eleven who died in the raid took place on the same day, December 14, 1940. It was, the paper reported: 'One of the most impressive spectacles in the history of the town'. The young Herbert Tucknott, who died at the Royal Sussex County Hospital in Brighton two days later, was buried with his family in Newhaven cemetery on December 23.

FRIDAY, JANUARY 17, 1941

On a very cold, sleety night, the wail of the sirens at 12.40am roused people from their slumbers, and as they hurried to the shelters the unmistakable dull thuds of bombs exploding close by could be clearly heard, together with the sounds of the local defence AA guns opening up.

Yet again, a single aircraft came in from the direction of the Channel, flying low. As it started to bank away, two high explosive bombs were seen to fall. One exploded at Sleepers Hole, the other, missing the harbour, exploded in the sea, about 50 yards to the south of the harbour mouth.

As the enemy aircraft crossed the town, bearing westwards, it opened up with machine gun and cannon fire, but caused only minimal damage. No injuries were recorded.

THURSDAY, MARCH 13, 1941

There was a bright silvery moon on this fine night when the townsfolk were alerted at 9.35pm by the noise of the local anti-aircraft guns. The sirens then signalled the start of the first air attack in almost three months, and the pips indicated that the enemy was overhead. By this time most had taken cover. It was a single aircraft and as its 500kg bomb began its fall machine gun bullets rained down, peppering roofs and breaking windows.

The bomb exploded in a gravel pit close to Gibbon Road. The blast caused extensive damage to about thirty homes. Four people needed hospital treatment, nineteen suffered minor injuries and another dozen or so suffered shock. Five families had to be evacuated and these were all temporarily re-housed with friends or relatives.

This was a lucky raid for Newhaven; residents still remembered the single 500kg bomb that had exploded in Folly Fields three months earlier, when twelve people lost their lives.

THURSDAY, APRIL 3, 1941

Newhaven people woke to a miserable day. It was raining and a thunderstorm rumbled overhead. Sunrise was at 6.31am and there were already some early-birds making their way to work.

The peace was shattered at about 6.53am when the sirens commenced their mournful dirge, quickly followed by both the 'pips' and the sounds of anti-aircraft fire. A Junkers Ju88 A-5 was seen approaching from the south west, with guns firing. The target was a goods train at North Quay. The Junkers dropped its load of four 500kg high explosive bombs. One struck the train, derailing some of the rolling stock. Another came to rest on the track. The third struck the ground close-by and broke in two, and the fourth exploded, causing serious damage to a number of military huts. Three people were taken to hospital, badly injured. This part of the railway system was closed for a few days. Two railwaymen were decorated for staying at their posts.

The Junkers, identified as 7208 of 5/KG1, also machine-gunned Seaford and was then attacked by two Spitfires and shot down into the sea off Seaford Head. See *Appendix 1*, CRASHED AIRCRAFT.

THURSDAY, MAY 15, 1941

At 3.50pm on a rather cloudy and chilly afternoon the sirens, together with the pips, announced the threat of an incoming enemy aircraft, believed to have been a Junkers Ju 88. It was soon seen approaching from the south west.

The Newhaven defence guns opened up, the Junkers dropped its load of four high explosive bombs in the sea some yards to the south of the breakwater, turned tail and fled back across the Channel. Minor damage was caused to a couple of nearby properties.

MONDAY, MARCH 23, 1942

At 5.55pm on this Monday afternoon, four Messerschmitt Me109s made a low level attack on the town. Each carried a high explosive bomb. They came in from the south east, on a straight flight path, and first attacked with machine gun and cannon fire. This was a lightning attack carried out with great determination.

Although the sirens had sounded, the aircraft arrived on the scene so quickly that there was barely time to reach the shelters. For many, it was a case of staying put, in any type of shelter that could be found from the deadly hail of bullets.

The aircraft released their bombs as they came in over the harbour area. The first bomb hit the marine offices at the southern end of the London and Paris Hotel. This bomb killed three people and injured six others, two seriously.

The second bomb exploded on the east side of the town beach, throwing up a great wall of pebbles. Another exploded harmlessly in the sea, to the east of

Newhaven Fort. The fourth exploded in Sleepers Hole. There were no casualties and no damage caused by this bomb. All 108 windows of the London and Paris Hotel were smashed and the hotel was very seriously damaged.

After the attack, which lasted just a minute or two, the raiders flew off out to sea. Several Spitfires appeared and headed off in pursuit. Shortly after they were out of sight gunfire was heard in the distance.

A man named Johnson was one of the three killed in the raid. He was probably a member of the services, as his name does not appear on a list of civilian casualties. The two other men

*Bomb damage to the marine
offices, London and Paris Hotel*

On March 23, 1942, bombs fell harmlessly on either side of the blockship SS Davarr. She was moored in the harbour entrance, to be sunk if an invasion were attempted. After the war the Davarr was broken up on the East Beach.

who died were railwaymen Frank Clark, fifty-one, of Brighton Road, Newhaven, and Charles Gates, fifty, of Railway Road, Newhaven. The body of Frank Clark was found in the debris on Tuesday evening. Some keys and a wallet containing the identity card of Charles Gates were found during the same day, and it is believed that his body was found later.

A O Johnson, age and address unknown
Frank Clark, 51, Brighton Road, Newhaven
Charles Gates, 50, Railway Road, Newhaven

TUESDAY, APRIL 28, 1942

What came to be known as 'the ten - second air raid' began at 10.24am when the sirens warned of an impending attack and two Messerschmitt Me109s came in fast and low, each carrying a single bomb. These were released and fell harmlessly in the sea near the mouth of the harbour. The explosions sent large water spouts skywards. The Messerschmitts then machine-gunned the town centre area, damaging roofs and windows, but although it was mid-morning on a bright sunny day, miraculously there were no casualties.

WRENS parade through Newhaven, passing Oxleys Corner,
for Wings for Victory Week, June 19-26, 1943

The aircraft turned eastwards, towards Seaford, still firing. This caused superficial damage to the brickwork of the cowshed at Foxhole Farm. The planes then turned south and quickly disappeared across the Channel.

This was the last recorded air attack on Newhaven during 1942; it would be more than a year before the next.

TUESDAY, AUGUST 17, 1943

Details of this attack (the only one recorded in 1943) are almost non-existent. The records state only that at 11.55pm on Tuesday, August 17, 1943, a single aircraft dropped one high explosive bomb on the golf course. No damage or injuries were recorded. There were no further details.

SATURDAY, MARCH 25, 1944

Soon after midnight the wailing air raid sirens filled the air and in just a few minutes the unmistakable sound of a German aircraft, almost certainly a Junkers Ju88A-4 was heard. The AA guns gave a good account of themselves, putting up plenty of flak, but the aircraft escaped damage and released more than eighty incendiary bombs, which fell around the harbour, lighting up the area as they burst into flames.

Most landed on Admiralty property, where a number of minor fires were caused but were quickly contained. Elsewhere more serious fires were caused, but again they were soon brought under control.

This was the last manned air attack on Newhaven during the war.

On this night London was the main target with 143 aircraft taking part. One had its fuel tanks punctured by AA fire over London, ran out of fuel on its return flight and crashed into the Channel, four miles south of Brighton at about 1am.

WEDNESDAY, JULY 6, 1944

A month had passed since D-Day, when allied troops stormed ashore at Normandy, and this lunchtime people were in relaxed mood, probably listening to the news on the wireless as they enjoyed their midday meal. The time was 1.04pm.

Annie Boyd tells the story: 'All of a sudden the guns started firing at an aircraft coming in from the direction of the sea. This plane appeared on fire with flames coming out at the back of it. It was a small plane and getting closer. I then suddenly realised that it wasn't a plane but a doodle-bug. I had never

Evening Standard

Morrison Announces New German "Air

PILOTLESS PLANES
RAID BRITAIN

ATCH THE LIGHT IN THE TAIL

The Ministry of Home Security offers the following advice to the public:
When the engine of the pilotless aircraft stops, and the lights at the end of the machine are seen to go out, it may mean that the explosion may soon follow, perhaps in fire to 15 seconds.
So take refuge from blast, even those indoors should keep out of the way of blast, and use the most solid protection immediately available

rule is NOW

'Counter-measures Are Vigorous'

The Germans have begun sending pilotless airplanes over this country. This was announced by Mr. Morrison, Home Secretary, in the House of Commons to-day.

THESE PILOTLESS AIRPLANES WERE USED IN THE RAIDS HERE LAST NIGHT AND TO-DAY. MR. MORRISON SAID:

It has been known for

'ALL ENEMY ATTEMPTS TO TAKE IN

ADVANCE OF
ACROSS P

THE ALLIED THREAT TO CUT TH IS INCREASING OUR TROOPS MILES EAST OF ST. SAUVEUR AND THE ROAD AT LA HAYE.

To-day's Allied communiqué reports but mentions the advance in the Penins have made further progress west of Pont l

seen one before, although I had heard about them. I didn't really expect to see one, except at the pictures. I knew that all the time you could hear it, it was all right, but if the engine noise stopped, then it was about to come down.'

'I watched it for a few seconds, then for some reason decided that perhaps I would get in the shelter. I hurried indoors, getting in the shelter. It went quiet, very quiet, it was so ghostly, although it was daylight. I can't really explain it, it gave me the shivers. I can remember that I didn't feel frightened, although maybe I should have done. This quietness seemed to go on for ever, and then – an almighty great bang. I think it was the loudest bang I have ever heard, it was incredible.'

This V1 – known as a doodle-bug, or flying bomb, crashed at Mount Pleasant where thirty houses were very badly damaged and another thirty less seriously damaged. Broken furniture was strewn on the road, garden walls were shattered and neat gardens were destroyed, making it difficult for the rescue services to reach the scene. By a miracle nobody was killed, and only thirteen people were hurt. Most of the injuries were cuts and bruises, but three people needed hospital treatment.

SATURDAY, JULY 30,1944

An explosion at about 3.40am at Burrow Head, Newhaven was, it is believed, caused by a V1 flying bomb. Fifteen houses were badly damaged.

TUESDAY, NOVEMBER 22, 1944

One of the largest explosions to occur in England during the Second World War happened at about 5am on this day. The end of the war was in sight, it had been months since an attack from the air and people were sleeping peacefully in their beds.

Di Simpson remembered the event well. 'I was living in Gibbon Road at this time. I was in one bedroom and the two kids in another. It was dark and suddenly, without warning, there was this almighty bang and I think there was another shortly after. The whole house shook very violently. In fact I was sure it was going to collapse on us. The clock fell off the mantlepiece, two large pictures fell off the wall and the front door was so twisted that we couldn't open it to get out. We had two ceilings down, four of our windows were broken and two others were cracked.'

'The children woke up screaming and rushed into my room. They were terrified – so was I. Our garden wall was strewn across the garden together with broken tiles from the roof.'

'This explosion was soon followed by loud voices out in the street as people started to spill out from their homes. I looked out of the front window and saw that the house across the road had no front door, one window was hanging out and another hanging loose. There were piles of rubble everywhere and the street was covered with broken glass and tiles.'

'We put coats on over our night clothes and ventured out after a while. The wardens came and one of them said that the town was a disaster area.'

The front of a Gibbon Road house was blown out by the huge blast when the ammunition barge blew up

Newhaven Harbour Station after blast damage from the barge explosion

'Anyway, we didn't get hurt, just shocked and frightened. I know that some people were hurt and had to go to hospital. More and more rescue people came up and gradually the street filled up with people. I was later told that a ship had been blown up by a mine.'

What in fact had happened was that a barge, loaded with more than 180 tons of high explosives, broke its towline during a storm and drifted ashore, passing the Fort.

Just to the west of this point the barge struck a mine and exploded in a blast that was felt up to ten miles away. Damage to property – smashed windows and broken roof tiles – occurred up to seven miles away.

One of the redeeming features of this incident was that the barge was beneath the cliffs of Castle Hill, which significantly helped to absorb the blast. But it was not enough to prevent hundreds of homes and business properties in Newhaven from suffering damage. The worst area was in and around Gibbon Road and the Hillcrest area.

A South Road resident said that even today there is still a crack in her house, caused almost sixty years ago when the ammunition barge went up.

Many people suffered from shock, and there were some with minor injuries. Incredibly, little more than half a dozen needed hospital treatment. Just one person was killed, a naval rating, who was crushed by a falling wall.

SEAFORD

Seaford, three miles to the east of Newhaven, and certainly not as strategically important, surprisingly suffered more from air raids than did the port town. In fact, apart from the two major towns either side, namely Brighton and Eastbourne, it suffered more during the war years than any other Sussex town. To many of the residents the six years of war seemed endless.

As in other seaside towns, many children were evacuated, and a number of residents sought shelter further inland, so casualties were not as high as they might have been.

In all, twenty-three people were killed, sixteen suffered appalling injuries and another eighty-four were slightly injured.

Twenty-eight houses and other buildings were completely destroyed, fifty-four were damaged beyond repair and eighty- two were damaged but salvageable. In addition, more than 1,900 other properties, mostly houses, suffered what was described as slight damage.

Forty- two incidents were recorded, including the thirty- seven air attacks. More than 140 high explosive bombs and countless incendiary bombs were dropped on Seaford.

Seaford children leaving home under the government's
voluntary evacuation scheme, July 1940.

WEDNESDAY, JULY 3, 1940

At 5.30pm on a pleasant summer afternoon the peace was shattered by the sound of the air raid siren. Seaford people, who had yet to experience their first air raid, were unsure if this were the real thing, but taught to treat every siren as real, they sought shelter.

When an incoming aircraft was seen the land defences opened up fiercely and the German crew immediately jettisoned their load of four high explosive bombs into the sea, some seventy-five yards from the shore line, mid-way along the seafront. The aircraft turned tail and headed back across the Channel.

About the same time as this raid, another aircraft was attacking a train, a little more than a mile away. It may be that this was the same plane, but research suggests that there were two aircraft, possibly from the same base.

SUNDAY, JULY 28, 1940

It was 11.45pm on a cloudless summer night when the sirens started to wail, and seemingly in no time the excrutiating cacophony of bombs landing and exploding was heard all over town.

The first fell on grassland close to the golf club north east of the town – well away from residential areas. Others fell and severely damaged houses towards the end of Kammond Avenue. Two elderly women in one of the houses had a miraculous escape, suffering only slight injuries. They were treated at the scene by local first aiders and were persuaded to go to the hospital for a check-up. After being discharged they returned to Kammond Avenue, but their home was unfit for occupation and they moved to friends living nearby. These two resourceful women captured everyone's imagination with their calm and cheerful manner, 'a lesson to all' someone was heard to remark.

Fetching in the milk

A local newspaper reported: 'The Civil Defence Services made a prompt turn-out, reflecting their complete state of preparedness and efficiency . . . When the explosions occurred, a number of people were guilty of looking out of their bedroom windows to discover what was happening – without turning out their lights.'

SUNDAY, AUGUST 18, 1940

At 12.40am a German aircraft crossed the coast at Cuckmere Haven and as it banked west the coastal defence guns opened up. The enemy straightened out and simultaneously released two high explosive bombs, which fell and exploded in a field at Chyngton Farm, west of Exceat Bridge. These bombs caused no injuries or damage. The aircraft made off back across the Channel, with the guns still firing.

THURSDAY, AUGUST 22, 1940

At 12.18am a German aircraft dropped two high explosive bombs on Seaford. The first fell on the Seaford Head golf course, causing a small crater but no other damage, and the second struck the garden wall of a house in Downend, and exploded in the garden. This caused considerable damage to the rear of a number of houses, and slight damage to houses backing on to the gardens. No injuries were reported.

THE SAME DAY

Seaford people, warned by the sirens, were in their shelters at 11pm when a single German aircraft dropped two incendiary bombs that set fire to gorse bushes on Seaford Head. Members of the Civil Defence were putting out the flames as members of the AFS arrived. There were no injuries and no damage, but there were a few jibes between the two services, which was to continue throughout the war years, just as it did elsewhere in England. Healthy rivalry was to the benefit of everybody.

MONDAY, AUGUST 26, 1940

Seaford Head was again the target when, at 1.19am, a single German aircraft dropped ten incendiary bombs, and once again the gorse was set alight, as was a large haystack, which blazed merrily and could be seen from miles away. Soldiers based nearby tackled the blazing gorse. The AFS were soon on the scene and quickly had the haystack fire under control. No serious injuries were reported, although one soldier suffered burns to his right hand and leg.

TUESDAY, AUGUST 27, 1940

The enemy returned at almost the same time the next day. Simultaneously the sirens and the pips were heard, and within a few seconds there were aircraft overhead and bombs falling. 'The explosions seemed to go on forever,' one Seaford woman remembered.

The aircraft, probably two, dropped fourteen high explosive bombs as well as several incendiary bombs – and yet again most fell on the golf course at Seaford Head. There were some military installations on the head, including look-out posts, and these may have been the targets. Gorse close to the links was set on fire again and there was some slight damage to windows and roofs of a house nearby. There were no casualties.

TUESDAY, SEPTEMBER 10, 1940

A single aircraft crossed the Channel at speed, coming in at 1.05am from the south east. Coastal guns opened up as it circled the town once, then dropped two high explosive bombs and two incendiary bombs. These all landed close together in a field near Firle Road. The bombs caused no damage or casualties.

MONDAY, SEPTEMBER 23, 1940

A few minutes after nine on this early autumn morning a single enemy aircraft dropped a stick of bombs on the town. One smashed into a house called Rosemary in Downsview Road; an occupant suffered a number of small injuries and was taken to hospital for treatment.

An incendiary bomb landed on waste ground at Sutton Avenue, causing no damage. Another bomb fell in Headland Avenue, causing minor damage, and four others, and another incendiary bomb, fell in the vicinity of Headland Avenue and Downsview Road. One failed to explode, and both roads were evacuated. The main damage occurred in Headland Avenue where both the gas and sewer mains were fractured.

THE SAME DAY

At 1.05pm the air raid sirens were again sounded to warn of impending danger. The raid that followed was one of sixty across the south east of England.

There was a watery sun and some breeze, indicating that summer was on the way out. Robert Braddick, of Moorfield, Headland Avenue, was busy in the garage before going in for lunch. A single German aircraft, flying in from the south west at a low altitude, swooped suddenly and dropped a stick of twelve small bombs; on this day, for the first time in Seaford, they brought death.

The target was identical to the one in the morning as the bombs struck properties in Headland Avenue and Downsview Road. In Headland Avenue, two houses were partially demolished – one was seventy-two-year-old Robert Braddick's home. He was killed instantly. His wife Ellen and their daughter were trapped under the debris for a while and were rushed to hospital as soon as they were rescued; they suffered serious injuries to their backs and legs.

In Downsview Road most of the damage was confined to broken windows and roof tiles. A number of trees were ripped up and garden fences were blown down. A fire was started in one of the houses but the prompt action of the wardens with stirrup pump and buckets of water soon put out the flames.

Robert Braddick, 72, Moorfield, Headland Avenue, Seaford

SUNDAY, SEPTEMBER 29, 1940

There is little detailed information about this particular air attack, which happened when an unidentified number of Messerschmitt Me109s swept in from the east. Attacks on shipping in the Channel were reported at around the same time. At about 4.40pm a couple of aircraft flew across Seaford and one dropped an incendiary bomb on Claremont Road, where it burst into flames as it hit the roadway. There was no damage or injury to people. This bomb was of the 2kg type. Immediately, it flew south across the Channel.

Shortly before this, at 4.25pm, a Hurricane (No P2677) was shot down in the Newhaven area by a Me109. It crashed in flames at New Road, Denton. The pilot, Sergeant A Edgeley, of 253 Squadron, based at Kenley, Surrey, baled out, landing at South Heighton with a shoulder injury. He was later admitted to the RAF Hospital at Halton. The aircraft was a write-off.

FRIDAY, OCTOBER 4, 1940

A single aircraft, hidden by low cloud, but heard in the town below, released four medium sized bombs that exploded in fields at New Barn Farm. The field had been set up with aircraft anti-landing traps and the bombs caused some damage to these. Apart from a few shattered windows and loosened roof tiles and slates in the farm buildings, there was no other damage.

SUNDAY, OCTOBER 27, 1940

On a cloudy, wet and miserable morning the traditional Sunday lie-in was disturbed at 8.15am by the familiar wail of the sirens, followed by the pips and then the drone of enemy aircraft. They were probably Junkers Ju88s, part of a large group, escorted by fighters, that simultaneously was mounting a fierce attack on Portsmouth and Southampton.

There was the sound of machine-gunning and the shattering of windows, then the bombs began to fall. The first exploded in the churchyard at St Leonard's, damaging and upturning tombstones. There was blast damage to neighbouring properties and two people were treated for cuts to the face and arms by a local first aid team.

The second bomb struck Seaford House in Steyne Road, causing considerable damage. This bomb was also responsible for the damage sustained to a garage in the same road, as well as to Steyne Cottage, which was being used by the War Office. A number of people were injured by this bomb, two of whom needed hospital treatment.

The third bomb landed in Marine Crescent, damaging roofs and windows, and fracturing the gas main. Flames shot high into the air, but the fire service and gas board workers soon had the situation under control. Here, three people suffered minor cuts.

The fourth bomb landed and exploded on waste ground adjacent to Fitzgerald Avenue. Another five high explosive bombs fell in the grounds of Seaford College, where five or six people were hurt; one needed hospital treatment. The college, too, was being used by the military.

A tenth bomb landed almost dead centre in Corsica Road, fracturing both the gas and water mains. Firemen and other rescue services were quickly on the scene but not before part of the roadway resembled a small river.

Nearby, a number of houses received slight structural damage, while a little further away the damage consisted mainly of the usual broken window and roof damage. The eleventh and final bomb struck Burdyke Lodge in Southdown Road. This caused considerable damage to the property and three people were injured – two with broken bones.

TUESDAY, OCTOBER 29, 1940

At 11.20pm on a cold, cloudy night, a single German aircraft, almost certainly a Messerschmitt Me109, swept in from the east and immediately began machine-gunning Seaford. Town centre properties had their windows cracked or broken and many roofs were damaged.

As the aircraft approached the Alfriston Road vicinity it released two high explosive bombs which struck land at Sunnyrise Nurseries and exploded. One greenhouse was completely demolished and another lost most of its glass. There were no injuries.

FRIDAY, NOVEMBER 14, 1940

No record was made of this raid, other than that it took place at 8.30pm and that one or, possibly, two oil bombs fell on Downland at Southdown Farm. One bomb fragment bore the letters *Flamc 500*. There were no reports of injuries or property damage.

SUNDAY, NOVEMBER 17, 1940

On a cold, but sunny afternoon, a Messerschmitt Me109 flew in low across the western part of town at 3.13pm. It crossed the coast near Claremont Road and a few seconds later was machine-gunning the village of Bishopstone. Two bombs were released, one exploding on Downland fifty yards east of Bishopstone Road. The other struck and exploded in Bishopstone Road, causing slight damage to the services. There was blast damage to roofs and windows and two people were treated for shock. The attack lasted only about twenty seconds and the aircraft turned and fled back across the Channel.

A party of 'defence diggers'. Volunteers came from all classes and ages. This group is gathered outside the White Hart Hotel in Lewes.

MONDAY, NOVEMBER 18, 1940

On a very cold, but clear morning, at 4.55am, Seaford people were woken by a cacophony of loud sounds. 'Everything seemed to happen at once; it was difficult to place the sounds in order; it was very frightening for everyone', said one resident who remembered that day well. 'I think it went something like this – first the local defence anti-aircraft guns in the seafront area were firing. Then, split seconds later, the wailing signals of the air raid siren, quickly followed by the pips.'

Possibly three aircraft were involved – or so the Civil Defence estimated afterwards. They flew in from a westerly direction and, after dropping their bomb loads, turned south and crossed the coast just east of Seaford Head, gathering speed across the water on the run home to their base in France.

The first three bombs to explode struck the football ground in Crouch Gardens, making large craters in the centre of the field.

Two more bombs fell in Bramber Road, one of them demolishing an unoccupied bungalow. The other struck the road surface causing blast damage to houses in the street.

A Mrs Marchant was already up, making tea in her kitchen, when the coastal guns, one less than a hundred yards from her home, started firing. She made it to the shelter just as the first bomb fell. 'There was a terrific bang. My house shook so much I was sure it was coming down on top of me. I have never heard such a noise. I was so frightened and afraid to move that I stayed there for what seemed hours.'

Another bomb fell in the back garden of a house in Heathfield Road. The blast from the explosion blew the chimney stack off the roof, and windows here and in other houses were shattered. Yet another bomb landed harmlessly in a field next to Fitzgerald Avenue, throwing up a huge wall of earth and grass. And three bombs landed in the roadway of the avenue, fracturing both gas and water mains. There was the usual gas fire accompanied by water gushing from a major breach of the main.

The next bomb exploded in Steyne Road, again fracturing gas and water mains. More bombs were dropped on the Downs at Seaford Head, including one high explosive bomb, one UXB and sixteen incendiaries.

Three people were treated for shock and six suffered minor injuries.

THURSDAY, DECEMBER 5, 1940

Two enemy aircraft crossed the coastline near Cuckmere Haven at 7.15pm, flying abreast. Although the local AA guns opened up the aircraft flew on undamaged. The sirens had given ample warning for residents to take shelter.

The aircraft released their loads and all eight bombs fell and exploded in a ploughed field about a mile to the east of Sunnyrise Nurseries in Alfriston Road. No serious damage was reported, and there were no injuries.

WEDNESDAY, DECEMBER 11, 1940

One enemy aircraft appeared suddenly, coming in from the Channel at fast speed, Three high explosive bombs were released, falling and exploding approximately 500 yards west of the Coastguard Cottages on Seaford Head. No damage was recorded.

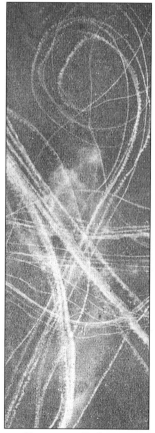

FRIDAY, JANUARY 10, 1941

An aircraft, almost certainly a Junkers Ju88, flew in low over the town shortly after midnight. It had been a cold day and night had brought rain and low clouds. Official records time this attack at 12.30am.

The aircraft crossed the coastline in the Cuckmere Valley area, passing over Seaford in a southerly arc, went back out to sea and returned, coming in around the Bishopstone area.

It dropped three high explosive bombs which all fell and exploded on land at Southdown Farm. This caused serious damage to two farm cottages as well as to outbuildings and cowsheds. There were no reports of any person being injured.

The aircraft then continued over the residential part of the town spraying machine gun bullets and cannon shells. Sutton Nurseries had fifty-three greenhouse windows shattered and the cemetery chapel had the stained glass windows damaged. In Sutton Park Road and Broad Street plate glass shop windows were broken.

The Haven in Vale Road lost its chimney stack and council houses in Vale Road sustained broken windows and roof tiles. Eleven houses in Alfriston Road, owned by Seaford UDC, were also damaged.

Vapour trails from a dog-fight over Seaford, December 1940

In Lexden Road, the front door at number 2 was shattered, and at number 4 the front windows were shot out. Slight damage was also caused in Belgrave Road, Chichester Road, Connaught Road, Cradle Hill, East Dean Rise, Hindover Road and Mason Road. An empty bungalow in Vale Road, number 70, was badly damaged.

A number of Junkers Ju88s of I/KG51 squadron had been despatched on special 'zerstoerungangriffen' (destruction attacks) against aircraft factories on this night. The targets were Hucclecote and Yate in Gloucestershire, and Glasgow West dry dock, but because of unfavourable weather alternative targets at Portsmouth, Bristol and the south east coast were bombed instead.

TUESDAY, APRIL 1, 1941

A low flying single aircraft came in from the east at 7.27am, dropped its load of four bombs, then turned, gaining height over Dane Road, and sped off, heading south west. The raid took little more than a minute or so, and left one man dead.

One bomb destroyed the Manor House in Broad Street, and another went through Turrel's Garage, out through the brick wall at the western end and across the churchyard, coming to rest outside the back door of The Plough, where it failed to explode.

The landlord's wife had been frightened by the raid, and her husband, to convince her that the enemy was gone, and all was now safe, led her to the back door, opened it and there saw the large UXB. Immediately everyone in the area was evacuated while a bomb disposal squad de-fused it and removed it later that afternoon.

Another bomb fell in Church Street, demolishing Kennard's Dairy. Alfred Boswell, fifty-four, was buried there beneath the rubble. In the shop next door Mrs Kent and her son and daughter were injured, although not seriously.

The fourth bomb exploded behind the Bay Hotel, causing considerable damage. Seven more people were injured in this incident and five needed hospital treatment.

The parish church suffered blast damage, several stained glass windows were destroyed and the clock face was wrecked.

One witness said that the machine came so low, and at such a pace that he thought it was going to crash. Another man said that he saw the raider approach from the east. It was diving at an acute angle and then seemed to straighten out for the bomb run.

Afterwards a warden found a small dog in a damaged and deserted house. It was covered with dust and dirt and was trembling violently. The warden handed it over to friends who cared for it until it could be returned to its owner.

In a local newspaper report of Alfred Boswell's funeral, which took place three days later, there was no mention that he had been killed by a German bomb. The report said that Mr Boswell, of Coniston, Alfriston Road, had died 'under tragic circumstances' at Kennard's dairy, where he had worked for more than twenty four years. He is buried in Seaford Cemetery.

> **Alfred William Boswell, 54, 37 Alfriston Road; at 41, Church Street**

THURSDAY, APRIL 3, 1941

Soon after 6.50am on this showery morning the sirens signalled an incoming aircraft – a Ju88-5 bomber that had, just minutes earlier, machine-gunned and bombed Newhaven.

The Junkers (No 7208), crewed by Oblt H Speh, Uffz J Gassen, Fw R Twartz and Fw J Mania, flew in low from the south west, machine-gunning as it came, then crossed the coastline a little to the west of Seaford Head, making off across the Channel.

Shortly afterwards it was intercepted by two Spitfires of 610 Squadron. All three aircraft headed out to sea and the Junkers was shot down, crashing into the sea about three miles off Seaford Head.

Speh and Gassen were reported as missing and the two other crew members were killed.

THURSDAY, APRIL 10, 1941

It had been a wet and miserable day with heavy rain and low clouds and many people were in bed when, at 10.20pm, the sirens issued their warning, followed by the pips.

Shortly afterwards the drone of enemy aircraft engines was heard. Although they were never seen, it was supposed that there were two aircraft that night. Four bombs were dropped and the planes turned and fled south, the raid lasting little more than half a minute.

The bombs fell in almost a straight line from seventy-five yards north east of the golf course in Firle Road, where two metal sheds were destroyed, in a north-easterly direction. This caused maximum damage to sixteen properties, including a school, in Chyngton Road; four in Links Road; ten in Rother Road; nine in Bracken Road; two in Arundel Road, and the senior council school; one in Cuckmere Road. A number of other homes were less seriously damaged.

WEDNESDAY, APRIL 16, 1941

It had been a fine and pleasant evening, with the sun setting at 7.57pm. At about 10.10pm the sirens wailed and two enemy aircraft swept in from the Channel. AA fire was ineffective, and the raiders commenced their bomb run. The first two bombs fell on Downland at Seaford Head, one causing slight damage to two military storage units. The other failed to go off.

As the aircraft crossed the town they dropped 500 incendiary bombs over a wide area, causing a number of small roof fires, two of which quickly turned into major fires. Three of these incendiaries failed to go off, and later were taken away for examination.

The aircraft also dropped two more high explosive bombs, which fell in Firle Road. One exploded in the grounds of Pilgrims School, while the other caused serious damage to a house called Roman Vale. At the school the roof was shattered, most of the windows were broken or cracked and there was severe shrapnel damage to the walls. Four people suffered injuries resulting from these two bombs. Damage was also caused to 6 Vale Road, 56 Sherwood Road, 39 Hartfield Road and a house named Bucklea in Marine Drive, Bishopstone. In total nineteen properties sustained damage in this attack.

SUNDAY, MAY 11, 1941

This particular night was cloudy and starless, with intermittent rain showers. Shortly after 12.40am the wail of the sirens stirred people from their slumbers and, by this stage of the war, well practised, knowing exactly what to do and where to go, they were quickly out of bed and on their way to the shelters.

Two high explosive bombs fell on land at Southdown Farm, exploding close to, and damaging, farm buildings. A cow was killed.

Another bomb fell and exploded on the playing fields at Bowden House, Firle Road, causing damage to the roof area. Many of the windows at the rear of the building were broken, due to the blast, scattering the glass over a wide area.This building was, at the time, occupied by the military. Two military vehicles were damaged.

THE SAME DAY

Just one aircraft, described in the local newspaper as a 'rogue raider', swept in over Bishopstone. Residents in the area had wondered for quite a few months if they would ever be a target. There were a number of military units stationed in and around the valley, and the Germans almost certainly knew this.

The sirens had sounded quite a while before and it was believed that the aircraft crossed the coastline to the west of Newhaven. It attacked the village from the north, machine-gunning, and dropping four bombs. Three exploded near Bishopstone House, causing extensive damage, and the fourth damaged Manor Farm Cottages and injured a cow, which was later destroyed.

Almost every building in the village sustained some sort of damage. Two small fires broke out but the residents soon had them under control.

The worst damage was at Bishopstone House where the roof was described as 'shredded'. Windows and window frames had been blown out, doors had been ripped off their hinges, bricks from the walls littered the roadway and inside the house the ceilings were either down or cracked.

The village church also suffered damage to the roof, and in The Vicarage ceilings were down, windows broken and a door blown off. The house was a wreck, but the vicar was seen helping villagers, with a smile on his face, encouraging the other residents.

An Anderson shelter damaged in a hit-and-run raid

In all, twenty-five properties suffered damage other than just broken windows. There were no serious injuries although the first aid teams treated villagers for cuts and shock.

THURSDAY, MAY 15, 1941

At 3.40pm on a cloudy afternoon a Junkers Ju 88 crossed the coast in the Saltdean area, turned and flew east, dropping six medium bombs at Beaufield, Tidemills, on grassland close to the coast road at Tidemills and close to a stud farm at Tidemills. Only the very slightest of damage was caused and there were no injuries.

This was the last air attack for 1941, and it was almost a year before the Seaford area suffered another raid.

TUESDAY, APRIL 28, 1942

Almost simultaneously with the sirens sounding a Messerschmitt Me109 flew in at low level, with machine guns blazing. It was 10.27am and there were many people out on the streets but, miraculously, only one was hurt, with a bullet wound in the leg.

As the aircraft passed over the town its bullets struck home, smashing windows and roof tiles. It was a terror raid, intended to panic the public, and was all over in just a few seconds.

The houses damaged were at 39 and 41 Vicarage Walk, 39 and 41 Sutton Road, 6, 25, and 26 Mercread Road, Waldronhurst in Grove Road and properties in Bramber Road, Claremont Road and Lexton Road. This was a forerunner for what was to happen six months later, almost to the day.

SUNDAY, AUGUST 9, 1942

People had been warned and were safely in their shelters – by this stage of the war many had Morrison shelters in their homes, while others had preferred to have Anderson shelters in their gardens – when, at 11.15pm, several German aircraft crossed the coast at Cuckmere Haven and turned westwards. The first bombs, seven in total, fell and exploded on farmland at Chyngton Farm. Only blast damage was caused – to a house called French Gardens in Chyngton Gardens. At the same time more than 700 incendiary bombs were dropped, causing many small fires.

Two high explosive bombs were dropped and exploded in Arundel Road causing damage to four properties; three fell on Cradle Hill Road causing very little damage and another single bomb fell on Bydown, a private school in Alfriston Road. The school was all but demolished and its ruins had to be pulled down. Another sixteen properties, including a post office and butcher's shop, were damaged. Debris was strewn over a wide area. As a result of this bomb, a short section of Alfriston Road remained closed for just over twenty-four hours.

As the aircraft crossed the town, machine-gunning, they dropped a further 1,200 incendiary bombs on the residential heartland of Seaford, setting homes on fire. Twenty-two houses in Hindover Road were damaged and three in Hindover Crescent. Vale Road had six damaged houses and other roads where damage was reported included Broad Street, East Street, Eastbourne Road, Grove Road, Guardswell Road, Heathfield Road, Mason Road, Meads Road, Pelham Road, Sutton Avenue and Sutton Drove. Once again the parish church was hit, this time by incendiary bombs and bullets.

This was a night when the fire service, the police and military units were at full stretch, and very thinly spread. It was almost a miracle that there were no deaths or serious injuries.

THURSDAY, SEPTEMBER 24, 1942

At about 1.25pm an enemy aircraft approached from the south east, coming in over Seaford Head. The raid began with a machine-gun and cannon fire attack on the military camp on the cliff-top. Ten men were hit, three sustaining very serious injuries. Two died later in hospital.

As the aircraft flew northwards two bombs were released, one landing and exploding on The Crouch football field. Several houses in nearby streets were damaged. The other bomb exploded in the grounds of Seaford College. One house was demolished, fifteen others were severely damaged and another eighty-four were slightly damaged. A number of people had to be evacuated.

The anti-aircraft guns opened up and witnesses saw smoke coming from the aircraft as it flew off across the Channel. No injuries were reported.

SUNDAY, OCTOBER 25, 1942

The attack from a single low flying German aircraft, that came in firing its machine guns at about 5.34pm, is remembered as the worst that Seaford suffered. Fourteen people died, twenty-six were injured and 422 properties were damaged. When the bombs began to fall the first struck and demolished 18 and 20 Broad Street – shops with flats above – where four people were buried in the debris.

Neighbours joined the rescue service in the painstaking digging and careful removal of a mountain of debris, aware that the condition of 16, next door (Mence Smith's, the ironmonger's), was so precarious that it could, at any minute, topple on top of them.

Several hours later they reached the trapped people. Two, James Gale, eighty-five, and his daughter, Fanny Gale, fifty-three, were already dead, but a Miss Lowe and her father were still alive, although seriously hurt. The same bomb injured another sixteen people, four of them seriously.

The second bomb fell on Sutton Road, the third on Sutton Park Road and a fourth on Vicarage Walk. The second bomb demolished 39 and 41 Sutton Road, and partly demolished 37. Six people were killed here. They were George Borissow, sixty-eight, and his daughter, Kathleen, thirty-four at 39 Sutton Road; Jessie Gamon Andrew, sixty-seven, at 39 Sutton Road; George Farnes, sixty-eight, at 41 Sutton Road; Kate Holcombe, sixty-eight, at 37 Sutton Road; Mary Willis, sixty-seven, from Hampton, Middlesex, at 39 Sutton Road.

This incident was particularly difficult for the rescue services as the road was almost completely blocked by the debris. It was believed that the bomb exploded just before reaching ground level. Mr Borissow was a keen bowler, and several of his woods were found in Broad Street, more than 200 yards from his home.

The bomb that dropped on Vicarage Walk killed two sisters, Fanny Buck, seventy-seven, and Mary Buck, seventy-one, who lived together in Cornford Road. Here the road was filled with debris from damaged buildings, and with furniture smashed to matchwood. Tattered curtains, ripped from windows, hung on trees like Christmas decorations.

Two others died from this bomb, Catherine Meeson, seventy-eight, at 41 Vicarage Walk, and Clara Smith, fifty-six, of Saxon Lane, who died at 39 Vicarage Walk.

In the vicar's report to the Civil Defence, he wrote: 'Vicarage damaged, Vicar and Family undamaged'.

The fourth bomb fell and exploded in Sutton Park Road causing extensive damage to many houses. The worst was at Mowbray, where the occupant was badly injured. Thirty-four houses and six flats in this road, as well as the Midland Bank, were damaged.

Other roads where damage occurred were East Street, Avondale Road, Broad Street and Church Road, where the school lost most of its windows.

Within a few seconds of the sirens' warning, warden William Tomley, fifty-four, was making his way to the control point at Crouch House. He was in Sutton Park Road, close to a house called Fairholme, when he found himself

Wrecked beyond repair – a house in East Street

The debris in Vicarage Walk

in the line of fire. A machine gun bullet struck him in the chest, and he was killed instantly. It was a further blow for the tragic Tomley family, for both Mr Tomley's sons had been killed while serving in the RAF.

One woman owed her life to her Morrison shelter. When the bombs began to fall she crawled inside and survived. Her husband and a friend, who stayed outside, died when their house fell on top of them.

In the wreckage of people's homes, rescue workers found unexpected items – a battery wireless still operating, a basin of eggs, unbroken. In the

Bomb-damaged property in Broad Street

remains of a kitchen they found the carcass of a pet rabbit that had been in its hutch in the garden. The rabbit's head and skin were found hanging over the clothes line outside.

There is no record of the fourteenth person who was killed in this raid.

James Gale, 85, 20 Broad Street
Fanny Gale, 53, 20 Broad Street
George Borissow, 68, 39 Sutton Road
Kathleen Borrisow, 34, 39 Sutton Road
Jessie Gamon Andrew, 67, 39 Sutton Road
George Farnes, 68, 41 Sutton Road
Kate Holcombe, 68, 37 Sutton Road
Mary Willis, 67, Hampton, Middlesex, at 39 Sutton Road
Catherine Meeson, 78, 41 Vicarage Walk
Clara Smith, 56, of Saxon Lane, Seaford at 39 Vicarage Walk
William Tomley, 54,
Fanny Buck, 77, Cornford Road, at 39 Vicarage Walk
Mary Buck, 71, Cornford Road, at 39 Vicarage Walk

THURSDAY, NOVEMBER 5, 1941

Soon after 12.30pm a Dornier Do 217 was heard approaching. The weather was atrocious. It was raining hard, the cloud ceiling was low and visibility was very poor – it was certainly not weather suited to a low level air attack.

The aircraft, flying extremely low, crossed the coastline about a quarter of a mile west of Seaford College then, as it started to climb away, discharged its load of four 500kg high explosive bombs. The plane had dropped its bombs at a height of just under 200 feet. It then turned westwards over the railway station and southwards back across the Channel.

The first three bombs all fell within sixty-five feet of each other, landing on terraced houses in Pelham Road. The height and direction of the Dornier caused the bombs to enter the houses at their rear and about three feet above ground level. The delay in fusing permitted them to reach the basements before exploding.

Five people died in the terrace, but for the number and size of the bombs, the damage to the property was considered quite small and the idea prevailed at the time that as the explosion chamber was confined and the debris load was more than that of the usual two storey property, the effects of the bombs were smothered. This then limited the radius of damage. The bombs penetrated

Pelham Road after the disastrous November 5 raid

very little below basement level, hence the absence of any earth 'shock' or any damage to the underground services.

The fourth bomb ricocheted off the concrete yard behind the Southdown Garage, damaging the council depot building, en route to exploding at the foot of the railway embankment. The distance from the garage to where the bomb exploded was 148 feet. It made a crater of approximately twelve feet in diameter and about six feet deep.

The Ritz cinema suffered damage to the roof, walls, windows and the large plate glass front doors. Properties in Clinton Place, Belgrave Road, Chichester Road, Church Street, Croft Lane, Vale Road, Broad Street and Westdown Road were damaged.

However, the main damage to life and property was caused by the first three bombs. At 11 Pelham Road, Flora Todd, eighty-one, had been sitting in her favourite green armchair close to the bay window. She often sat there, looking out of the window, or reading. As the first bomb exploded, bringing the building down, she was buried beneath tons of debris, and died immediately.

The bodies of four other people were recovered from the basement areas of nearby collapsed houses.

Beneath the rubble that had been 10 Pelham Road a woman was trapped for five and a half hours. Large pieces of wooden furniture had created a 'tent' above where she lay, giving her a little space, and air. She suffered shock, bruising and several small cuts, was treated at the scene and went home.

At the other end of the terrace was Lloyds Bank where two members of staff managed to get down the stairs to the safety of the basement, which was used as the strong room. The bank suffered only superficial damage.

The basement of 14 Pelham Road had been fitted with blast walls at the door and window. A Morrison shelter was also installed, and was situated just twelve feet from the point of the exploding bomb. Although this shelter was slightly displaced, it was otherwise found intact.

The rescue services excelled themselves. They worked through to the following Sunday, when the last body was recovered.

Gordon Marsh, a transport clerk, was working for Hall and Company, coal merchants, at the railway goods yard. He recalled that November 5 was wet and damp, unpleasant to work in.

'I can remember clearly hearing the drone of an enemy aircraft. We were used to the different aircraft engine sounds, they were so different that by this time it was fairly easy to tell. I couldn't see the plane because of the mist. Apart from the droning of the aircraft, it was otherwise sort of quiet, a little strange, I guess. At this stage I thought I had better make for the air raid shelter, but I suddenly decided against it and instead sheltered in one of the very large coal containers. The droning got louder and as I looked up this massive German plane flew right over the top of me. It was so low it was barely above the roof tops. I could see the Germans in the plane, in fact had I had a brick with me, I am sure I could have thrown it and hit them.

After it passed over all hell was let loose, small pieces of debris started to rain down, from all directions. When I emerged the whole area seemed so dark, even though

The council depot in the station goods yard

68

it was the middle of the day. The air was filled with dust, dirt and little parti-
cles – clouds and clouds of this stuff seemed to be rolling around.'

'It wasn't long before I realized that the street opposite, Pelham Road, had
been bombed. I could see that some houses near the top of the road were a
pile of rubble, and another house, although standing, was dangerous. It was all
so sudden and unexpected. I later found out that a bomb had virtually passed
over me, in the coal yard. It struck the corner of a large building, which was
used for stores and took a large piece of concrete out of the corner. Later I saw
a groove in the ground where the bomb had struck before hitting the building.'

'I can't remember if anyone was killed but later I did hear that a young girl,
Betty Hamper, was trapped beneath the rubble. She was eventually rescued,
and was badly hurt. I can recall seeing her around the town over the years. I
don't think she ever got over her serious injuries.'

Alfred Cosham, then a ten-year-old boy, was at school in Church Street, having his midday meal when the bombs fell. The dining area, he said, was
strewn with glass and debris.

'We had just had our dinner and were having our pudding. I won't forget it
as my favourite dish was about to be served. Huge trays of custard tart were
about to be dished up when the bombs fell. I know we were only yards away
from being killed, but never realised it at the time. In those days a fair propor-
tion of children went home for their dinner but on this day there were around
eighty staying for dinner.'

'We were all dismissed about 2pm owing to the amount of damage that had
been caused. I helped the WVS ladies who had set up a refreshmnent bar in an
empty shop in Dane Road. We served ARP wardens and other rescue workers.
We also served the many lorry drivers who were removing the rubble and
debris. They were from the Eastbourne firm Avann.'

In 1942 Betty Hamper was fifteen years old and worked as a junior clerk for
Fuller and Cooper, the solicitors, in Pelham Road. One of the sticks of high
explosive bombs that fell on November 5 demolished the building where she
worked, turning it into a massive pile of rubble.

Betty was buried alive but, by sheer luck, a bath from the flat above the
office somehow covered her head and face, allowing her to breathe. Betty,
badly hurt and in terrible pain, was trapped for more than six hours before rescue workers reached her.

Not knowing if she were alive or dead, the team toiled on throughout the
afternoon and at about 6pm they heard her muffled cries for help. Dr Mary
Ryan managed to crawl through the remaining rubble and to treat her with
pain killing drugs.

Those who were there were astonished that Betty could smile and make light

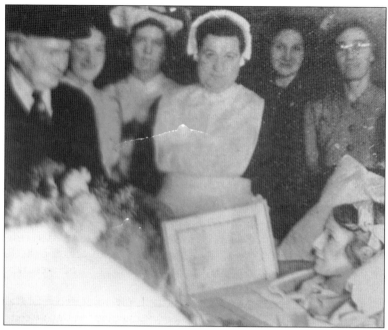

Betty Hamper in hospital, with her Certificate of Merit

of her pain. Eventually, around an hour later, she was lifted from the wreckage and rushed by ambulance to the Royal Sussex County Hospital in Brighton. Large pieces of flesh had been torn from her back, an arm and a leg and it was considered a miracle that she had survived with such injuries, entombed under the rubble, dirt and debris.

Betty, a member of the 1st Blatchington Company of Girl Guides, was still in hospital two months later when Dame Alice Godman, the County Commissioner of Sussex Girl Guides, surprised her with the presentation of the Guides' award for bravery, a Certificate of Merit.

Betty's horrific injuries disabled her for the rest of her life and she was never able to work again. She died of cancer in Seaford in 1979. Her ashes were scattered on her mother's grave in Seaford Cemetery.

The official records show that on this November 5, five people were killed, two seriously injured, four slightly injured, six houses demolished, a seventh so badly damaged that demolition was necessary, 198 houses slightly damaged and five other buildings damaged.

This may not have been Seaford's worst air attack, but it was certainly close to it.

Annie Louisa Cook, 79, Central Building, Sutton Park Road,
at 14 Pelham Road
Cilda Daphne Fort, 26, 14 Pelham Road
Harriet Martin, 68, 4 Pelham Rise, at 14 Pelham Road
Florence Perkins, 29, of Lenham Avenue, Saltdean, at 14 Pelham Road
Flora Ellen Todd, 81, 11 Pelham Road

WEDNESDAY, JANUARY 20, 1943

Just before 1pm two aircraft were spotted coming in from the Channel. The sirens were sounded as two Focke-Wulf 190s, flying abreast, came in low, crossing the coastline just to the east of Dane Road, with machine guns blazing. The raid lasted for just seconds.

Minimal damage was caused to property but two people were hit by machine gun bullets. One, a man, was hit in the chest as he ran across Dane Road, seeking shelter. The second, a woman, was hit on the arm. Both were taken to hospital for treatment.

Several War Office properties were damaged, including those at 4 and 6 Grosvenor Road, one in Claremont Road and yet another in Dane Road. The Rectory and other property in Belgrave Road was also hit.

The tenant of 163 Vale Road complained when her home was struck by machine gun fire. It had been hit in a raid ten days earlier. She said that damage had been repaired only two days earlier and she was convinced that there was some sort of vendetta against her, saying that she was sure that Hitler had her address.

Other streets where damage to properties occurred included Church Lane, Edinburgh Road, Newhaven Road, Tudor Close and Westdene Road.

SUNDAY, MARCH 14, 1943

A Messerschmitt Me109 appeared over the town at 12.30am and commenced a machine gun and cannon fire attack. The raid lasted seventeen seconds and records show that only one house suffered slight damage.

At daylight, nine cannon shell cases were found in town centre streets.

Later the same morning, soon after 10am, George Langridge of 30 Brooklyn Road went to the police station and handed over a live shell which had penetrated his sitting room window. Subsequently another eight shells were handed in.

TUESDAY, AUGUST 17, 1943

At midnight a single German bomber crossed the coast just west of the Martello Tower. The sirens had already sounded giving residents time to take shelter. There had been fewer raids in the past year or so and some had become a little blasé about acting immediately.

Almost as soon as the plane was over the town it released two bombs. One hit and demolished a disused laundry in East Street and two adjoining unoccupied houses. Three other properties were so badly damaged that they had to be demolished and thirty homes nearby were classed 'seriously' damaged. Many people were trapped and the rescue workers were again put to the test. Alongside the Civil Defence, police, military and other teams who toiled throughout the night were the women of the WVS with their welcome tea wagon. East Street was cordoned off for two days while a mountain of rubble and debris was cleared.

Records do not show the location of the second bomb, which caused damage to 100 properties, mainly houses, and a number of military vehicles.

NOTES FROM THE WAR RECORDS

At 11.45am on Monday, October 14, 1940, Lt Niel of the 7th Devon Regiment found a dead male body close to the water's edge on the beach at Cuckmere. It was clothed only in uniform trousers, which contained a wallet with identity papers bearing the name Henrich Luckhardt. He was a feldwebel, 27 years old, born in Mannheim, Germany. An identity disc, with the number 17/B65105 was also found. Henrich Luckhardt was buried at Seaford on Wednesday, October 16, 1940.

At 6.50am on Thursday, April 3, 1941, an enemy aircraft, flying at a low altitude, machine-gunned the town but there were no casualties, and no damage was reported. At 6.55am the aircraft was attacked by two Spitfires out to sea. A Mr Wilkinson reported seeing the enemy aircraft crash into the sea. Later a Junkers 88 was reported to have been shot down by two Spitfire pilots.

At 8.50am on Monday, April 12, 1943, a Mr Garnett of Speedwell Patch, Surrey Road, reported finding an unexploded shell on the fairway of the sixteenth hole at Blatchington Golf Course. It had penetrated the turf to a depth of approximately two feet.

At 3pm on Monday, November 15, 1943, two anti-tank beach mines were found at Cuckmere Haven. The area was cordoned off and the mines dealt with by 613 Company, Royal Engineers, stationed at Bowden House, Firle Road, Seaford.

At 1.30pm on Sunday, February 8, 1944, the occupier of 27 Chichester Road reported a broken window. A pane of glass in a north-facing upstairs window was broken by a shell splinter.

At 12.30am on Thursday, June 18, 1944, LAC Haberfield, RAF unit, stationed at Seaford reported that he saw two men in the sea off Seaford Head in a dinghy. After repeated shouts, a call for help was heard coming from the direction of the sea. There was one man in the dinghy, an American airman. He was Captain Luther Rolls Williams, of 397 USAAF Base, HQ Rivenhall. He was rescued and taken to the Naval Sick Bay, East Quay, Newhaven. His aircraft had run out of fuel while he was preparing to land at Friston airfield and he crashed into the sea. He said that some crew members got out of the aircraft but not all. After being in the water for a time, he drifted away from the others. A search was made for the other crew members without success.

At 9.30pm on Friday, July 24, 1944, a flying bomb was seen travelling at speed over Seaford in a northerly direction. The Ack Ack guns went into action and a fighter aircraft also attacked it. During this action, a Canadian soldier, L/Cpl Brenner of 30th Tank Troop Workshops, REME, at Bishopstone, and Gordon Parks, fourteen, of 156, Vale Road, suffered injuries from flying shrapnel. The roof of 4 Blatchington Road was penetrated by a canon shell, causing slight damage.

At 9am on Tuesday, December 10, 1946, a Mr Shutter, a railway sea defence worker, found a British landmine on the beach at Bishopstone, above the high water mark. At 3.45pm it was rendered safe by a detachment of the Bomb Disposal Section from Southwick.

DECOY LIGHTS AND COASTAL DEFENCES

Much has been written about the the coastal area of Sussex as it was during the Second World War – the devastating air attacks, for instance, the large military concentrations in seaside towns and on the Downs, the role of the rescue services, how the populace coped, in cold homes, on short rations and often in fear of their lives.

However, there is little or no mention about coastal defences and, although this chapter is far from being fully detailed, it will give readers some idea of the network of gun emplacements (and other measures) set up along the coast to repel the enemy.

Decoys were widely used during the 1939-45 war to mislead and deceive the enemy. Bogus airfields were created, with sham airfield buildings and Hurricanes and Spitfires made from cardboard or thin wood indicating a flight or squadron of aircraft on a fighter airfield. Then there were decoy 'fires', used by both civilians and the military to represent buildings that had been bombed – so acting as a marker for following waves of bombers. Other 'fires', carefully controlled, were used close to large towns and cities, simulating vast buildings blazing.

In 1942 a scheme to erect night-time decoy lights in the area of the meanders of the Cuckmere estuary was considered – to fool German bombers into thinking the Cuckmere Haven area, which was empty of all habitation bar a row of coastguards' cottages, was in fact the Ouse valley and Newhaven harbour.

When military heads received the detailed plans there was immediate disagreement. The Army and the Navy were very much for the scheme which could save shipping in the harbour from enemy attack. But the RAF objected to the lights. The two principal reasons given were that the Luftwaffe would not be fooled, and that Cuckmere Haven was too close to the fighter airfield at Friston. And Gayles Farm, on the flat top of the first of the Seven Sisters, was an advanced fighter airstrip. (Gunner Bob Truelove remembered a fire power demonstration on Seaford Head when he was firing Bren guns on fixed lines at bushes on the opposite side of the estuary. Two Spitfires flew straight in from the sea, through the tracer, and landed at the airstrip.)

Two sites were selected for the decoy lights, north and south of Exceat Bridge, but after many meetings between the War Office, the military authorities and the GPO it was agreed to drop the northern site and concentrate on the southern one. Finally the decision was taken to go ahead and the lighting system at Newhaven was faithfully copied, including a representation of the railway line from Newhaven to Lewes. The plan was for the decoy lights at

Cuckmere to be switched on whenever the air raid sirens sounded after dark. The control panel was situated close to where the Golden Galleon pub stands at Exceat Bridge.

There are many views on whether this system was successful. Newhaven suffered many air attacks during which people were killed and buildings reduced to rubble, but not much happened at Cuckmere Haven. Another view is that Hitler did not want the harbour at Newhaven damaged as it was destined to be an invasion port to unload his troops.

On March 13, 1945, the Regional Civil Defence office stated that the Cuckmere Haven decoy site had been removed.

Along the coastal strip between Brighton and Seaford were a number of defensive gun sites. Two were situated in the Ditchling Road area of Brighton, one being just north of Barnett Road and the other opposite Hollingbury Copse. Both were 40mm Bofor light anti-aircraft guns manned by the Army. The gun crews were billeted at 94 Barnett Road.

There were also gun sites on Marine Parade, one near the Aquarium, one near the junction with Lower Rock Gardens and another further east at the bottom of Paston Place. These were also 40mm Bofors capable of firing 120 two pound proximity fused shells per minute. They could reach a height of some 13,500 feet. The guns were of British manufacture to an original Swedish design. Each of the sites had a crew of five men consisting of a sergeant in charge, two gun layers and two men to feed the ammunition.

These Brighton seafront guns were manned by both British and Canadian

A battery of 3.7 inch heavy anti-aircraft guns

75

soldiers. Many of the Canadians were billeted in the Kemp Town area and assisted the Civil Defence in a number of rescues of bombed and blitzed premises in the town.

During the first week in June 1943, the 39th Light Ack Ack (AA) Regiment took up station in the East Brighton area and established batteries along the coast from the Roedean area west to Lancing. There was a large six inch naval gun in the gardens at Lewes Crescent, camouflaged by the trees and bushes at the southern end. On the first occasion that this gun was fired it blew out a number of nearby windows. Later the gun was moved to another site away from residential properties.

A 40mm Bofors was sited at the eastern end of the Gardens – the walkway between Marine Parade and Madeira Drive. This was handily placed in 1944 to combat the menace of the V1 rockets (doodle-bugs). The crews of these two gun sites were billeted in nearby Sussex Square and the two sites were linked by the underground tunnel beneath Marine Parade.

The third battery, consisting of a number of light anti-aircraft guns, spread eastwards from Brighton. There was a unit near Rottingdean golf course, north of the windmill, and another was in Whitehawk Hill Road, an unmade-up track running northwards from Abbey Road, near the Royal Sussex County Hospital. This was close to the radar station, where the television transmission mast now stands. It was a well sited unit that commanded an extensive view of the East Brighton area as well as the Channel.

A little known gun emplacement was just above a small wooden storage building on the football pitch in Whitehawk Road. The gun was a 20mm His-pano cannon, the same as those mounted in the wings of wartime fighter air-craft. It had a sixty-round drum and in a three second burst could fire ten pounds weight in fire. It was on a simple swivel and elevating mounting, which the gun-layer moved manually via a double shoulder mounting. The gun was sited to fire horizontally over the roof tops of Whitehawk homes, and was specifically placed to attack the tip-and-run raiders who crossed the Channel at little more than wave-top height, rise as they crossed the coast, fly low up the Whitehawk valley, bank near the top and sweep down and across the main town, releasing bombs and firing their weapons, before escaping out to sea.

To counteract this, two Lewis guns were sited at the top end of the valley, just south of the racecourse. The position of these guns allowed them to fire straight down the 'throats' of the German aircraft as they came up the valley. The guns were of .303 inch calibre on a single mounting, and both were equipped with 100-round drum magazines.

There was also a mobile gun in the racecourse area. This was a Beaverette

Coastal defences near Peacehaven.

light armoured car with an open turret. There were two Vickers K 100-round drum aircraft machine guns mounted on the vehicle, again of .303 inch calibre. The vehicle used to patrol up and down on the eastern side of the racecourse, from the top of Manor Hill to the tunnel that runs under the course.

A small gun was mounted on top of Marine Gate, the block of flats at Black Rock that was the most heavily hit of all Brighton buildings during the war. In May 1943 when the building was bombed one of the two man crew was killed and the other badly wounded.

The Roedean pitch and putt course was the site of Brighton's largest AA guns. These were a battery of four guns, each of 3.7 inch calibre. They were at the eastern end of the course, close to the junction of Marine Drive and Roedean Road. The guns fired twenty pound proximity fused shells to about 40,000 feet.Quite often they were aided by radar with targets being telephoned through. But more usually they used sound location to pinpoint targets. This consisted of a set of cones, rather like giant ear trumpets, that could pivot and elevate. The cones would locate the aircraft and determine its height, speed and course. The information would be fed to a predictor which would work out where to fire the guns and also what fuse setting to employ, in order that shell and aircraft met.

The Bofors and the 3.7 guns were manned by the Royal Artillery (and there were also ATS on the Roedean site) while the 20mm cannon, the machine gun post and the Beaverette were all manned by the RAF Regiment.

In Wilson Avenue 40mm Bofors were situated at regular intervals from top to bottom. Local children took much-appreciated food and drink to the crews,

The radar site at Portobello.

and in return were allowed to 'play' on the guns.

Roedean School was taken over by the navy. It was renamed HMS Vernon and used as a training base for torpedo gunners and electrical engineers. The practical side of the training took place in garages at the Grand and Metropole hotels where mock-up sites were built.

There was a .303 Lewis gun on the roof of the recently-built St Dunstan's Home for the Blind, at Ovingdean. Here, one afternoon, the sailor due to take the afternoon watch arrived the worse for drink. He took his position on time but after a few minutes he decided that he would benefit from some gun practice. Naval personnel at Roedean, next door, were on parade and were startled when the St Dunstan's gun began firing. They were even more startled when the gunner swung the gun around, still firing – and they dived for cover. The drunken sailor was arrested and taken away.

At Rottingdean there was a light AA gun site north of the village and east of the Falmer Road, and there was also a 40mm Bofors at the souther end of the village, west of the High Street.

A heavy AA site was situated at the southern end of Saltdean, close to the Lido. This unit was responsible for shooting down a Dornier Do 217 at 4.30pm on February 10, 1943, as it returned from a raid on Newbury in Berkshire. The aircraft crashed behind Homebush Avenue in Saltdean, with no survivors.

A radar installation – officially called Newhaven Radar Site – was situated on the cliffs at Peacehaven, close to Portobello. It was manned by the Army. At the eastern end of Peacehaven, about half a mile north of the Brighton Road, there was a heavy AA 3.7 inch gun.

The area now known as Rushy Hill Caravan Park was an army camp in 1942, the base of the South Lancashire Regiment. The various gun sites here included a heavy 3.7inch, 40mm Bofors guns and a machine gun post. A quarter of a mile eastwards towards Newhaven, at High View Lodge, were a searchlight and a barrage balloon position.

Terry Hawkins lived with his family at The Leas, Peacehaven, overlooking the caravan park during the war years, and as a young boy would often watch the gun crews at practice. Normal drill would be for a Lysander from Shoreham airfield to fly past trailing a 'sock' type target for the gunners to aim at. After the practice the pilot cast off the 'sock' which was collected by ATS girls who carted it away to record the number of hits on the target, and the accuracy of the gunners.

Terry remembered a twin Vickers gun being taken towards the cliff edge and screwed on to a concrete mounting. The crews used this gun to practice firing at gas filled balloons.

In 1940 three Navy six inch guns were installed on Castle Hill, Newhaven, west of the Fort, where there were already two other six inch guns, two twelve-pounder AA guns and a light AA gun. The battery consisted of three concrete roofed emplacements, each with magazines attached. There was a command post at the rear, further down the hill. Later the guns at Newhaven Fort were controlled by the radar site at Portobello.

The six inch gun at Newhaven Fort.

Appendix 1

CRASHED AIRCRAFT

On April 3, 1941, a Junkers 88A-5, No 7208, was shot down by Fl Lt Morris and Sgt Ballard in two Spitfires of 610 Squadron at 6.57am and crashed into the sea about three miles off Seaford Head. The crew did not survive.

On April 10, 1941, a Heinkel HE 111H-5, No 3592, was shot down at 10pm by F/O Eric Barwell DFC and Sgt Martin in a Defiant of 264 Squadron. This aircraft crash-landed at Blatchington Golf Course, Seaford. The pilot, Lt K Conrad, landed the blazing aircraft among anti-invasion wires and was captured. Three other crew members baled out and were taken prisoner. The fifth member of the crew baled out but his parachute failed to open and he was killed.

On Saturday, March 25, 1944, a Junkers Ju885-1, No 301228, was hit by AA fire over London. With its fuel tanks punctured it made its way southwards but at 1am it ran out of fuel and crashed into the sea about four miles south of Brighton. The bodies of the crew members, including the pilot, were found and buried at sea. Another crew member baled out and was captured in a one-man dinghy soon after 5am the same day.

Appendix 2

AIR RAID PRECAUTIONS

Before the war began the Home Office issued every householder with a little booklet entitled *The Protection of Your Home Against Air Raids*. This explained about the importance of the blackout – the darkening of every window, skylight or glass door with thick curtains or blinds so that enemy aircraft should not see any lights at night. The booklet also described how to create a refuge room.

The best place for such a room was a cellar or basement. It was a place easy to reach and to get out of, where people could be reasonably safe during an air raid. They were advised to stock the room with candles and matches, an electric hand lamp, tins and jars of food, drinking water, chamber pots and toilet paper (with a screen for privacy), a bottle of disinfectant, first aid supplies, books, toys for the children, spare blankets and mattresses and a wireless set.

The refuge room had to be sealed against the entry of gas, and the way to do it was to fill in all cracks and crevices with putty or a pulp made from sodden newspaper. Cracks in walls and ceiling had to be papered over, and cracks in the floorboards also needed to be filled.

Ventilators had to be stopped up with rags or pasted over with thick paper. Windows also had to be sealed and wedged firmly in their frames, and the panes covered with thick brown paper.

Advice on choosing your refuge room, – on a Churchman's cigarette card.

All doors which need not be used had to be sealed, and the remaining door had to have, on the outside, a blanket fixed securely to the frame with just a flap to get in and out of the room. If the blanket were kept damp during the air raid it gave better protection. For extra safety, wooden props could be fixed to support the ceiling.

In a sealed refuge room ten feet by ten feet, five people could remain in complete safety for twelve hours, without ventilation, the booklet said. The arrival of Anderson and Morrison shelters lessened the need for refuge rooms. The booklet also advised householders to clear the loft, attic or top floor of all flammable material and to protect the floor with sheets of corrugated iron, sheet iron or asbestos wallboard, or failing that, with two inches of sand.

Appendix 3

CHRONOLOGY OF THE 1939-45 WAR

<u>**1933**</u>	Adolf Hitler became Chancellor of Germany
<u>**1935**</u>	Prime Minister Stanley Baldwin's government issued a circular on air raid precautions (ARP)
<u>**1937**</u>	Air Raid Warden service created

<u>**1938**</u>

August
Formation of Women's Voluntary Service (WVS)
Building of Anderson shelters commenced (named after
Sir John Anderson, the then Home Secretary

September
ARP services mobilised
Gas masks issued
Plans put into force for mass evacuations
First barrage balloons raised over London

November
Schedule of reserved occupations issued

<u>**1939**</u>

February
Anderson shelters issued to the public

June
Women's Land Army formed; three and a half million
people evacuated from cities

August
Lord Haw Haw (William Joyce) offered his services
to Josef Goebbel's Nazi Ministry of Propaganda
Trial blackout in London (9th)
Censorship imposed on overseas mail (24th)
Emergency Powers (Defence) Act passed, enabling the
government to introduce regulations without reference to
Parliament (24th)

September
Start of blackout and of official evacuation (1st)
Declaration of war (3rd)
Sirens heard for the first time (3rd)
Introduction of National Service Act (3rd)

Winston Churchill appointed First Lord of the
 Admiralty (3rd)
British Ministry of Information formed
First broadcast of *ITMA* on radio (19th)
National Register introduced – everyone issued with
 an identity card (29th)

October   Dig for Victory campaign began
Churchill proposed establishment of units of Local Defence
 Volunteers (LDV), later to be known as the Home Guard

November   Introduction of possible deferment of individual workers
 in key occupations

December   Evacuees went home for Christmas
By the close of the year there were 43,000 women in nursing
 and women's services

1940

January   Two million British men, aged 19-27, were called up (1st)
BBC introduced the Forces programme
Food rationing began (8th); initially butter (4oz each
 per week), sugar (12oz) and bacon (4oz)

March   Meat was rationed

April   Vera Lynn was voted the British Expeditionary Force's
 (BEF) favourite singer

May   Tea was rationed
Churchill became Prime Minister (10th)
Anthony Eden, War Secretary, appealed for men to
 join the Home Guard (14th)
The Home Guard began patrolling the streets (15th)
Start of the evacuation of the BEF from Dunkirk (27th)

June   The BBC began broadcasts of *Music While You Work*
Churchill made 'We'll fight them on the beaches'
 speech (4th)
Italy declares war on Britain and France (10th)

July   Margarine and other fats rationed. Free or cheap milk

made available for mothers
Ministry of Supply made salvage collecting compulsory
Hitler planned Operation Sea Lion, the invasion
  of Britain (21st)

August
The Home Guard affiliated to Army county regiments
Battle of Britain reaches its height (15th)
Icing on wedding cakes banned

September
Commencement of the Blitz on London (7th)
Buckingham Palace bombed (13th)
The RAF win the Battle of Britain (15th)
Evacuation of children from cities started again (28th-29th)

October
Princess Elizabeth and Princess Margaret broadcast to
  evacuees on BBC Radio's *Children's Hour*

November
Coventry blitzed (14th)

December
Sale of silk stockings became an offence

1941

February
Official figures state that 1,370,000 children and women
  billeted as evacuees
Cosmetic rationing began, except for lipstick

March
The Lend Lease Bill passed in the USA enabling America
  to send supplies to Britain

April
Women's services became part of the Armed Forces

May
The last, and worst night of the Blitz (10th)
First of the Lend Lease supplies arrive in Britain

June
Clothes rationing and the Utility scheme for retail
  goods started
Venereal disease rate increased by 70% in two years
Official figures released on 19th show that two million
  houses had been destroyed or damaged, 60% of which
  were in London

November
Points rationing on food introduced

December	Japan attacked Pearl Harbour; the USA entered the war (7th) Allied losses during the Battle of the Atlantic was 195 ships

1942

January	First of the GIs (US servicemen) arrive in Britain (26th)
February	Food rationing extended
May	Introduction of Utility clothing
July	Churchill survived vote of 'no confidence' in the Commons
August	Churchill met Stalin in Moscow (12th) Duke of Kent killed in a plane crash in Scotland (25th)
October	Battle of El Alamein Extension of fuel rationing; baths to contain no more than five inches of water
December	Beveridge Plan proposed far reaching social reforms (1st) Points rationing extended

1943

January	Churchill and Roosevelt met in Casablanca and issued a demand for unconditional surrender by Germany
March	Bethnal Green tube disaster; 173 crushed to death (3rd)
June	King George VI visited troops in North Africa; awarded George Cross to Island of Malta
July	Age limit for conscription for women raised to 50, but those with family responsibilities were exempt Vigorous campaigns for National Savings
August	Home Guard numbered 1,100 regiments, consisting of 1,750,000 men

1944

March	The RAF acknowledged use of 12,000lb bombs in raids on German cities (3rd)

Seventy-nine Allied airmen escaped from Stalag Luft III prisoner-of-war camp

May   The Butler Education Act came into force

June   D-Day (Allied troops invade Normandy) (6th)
                First attacks by V1 flying bombs (doodle-bugs) on London

September   First attacks by V2 weapons

October   Churchill and Stalin met in Moscow

1945

February   Churchill, Roosevelt and Stalin engaged in Yalta Conference

March   Princess Elizabeth joined the ATS
                Allied troops crossed the Rhine

April   Death of President Roosevelt
                Russian troops reached Berlin
                Hitler committed suicide in his Berlin bunker

May   Germany surrendered (7th)
                VE (Victory in Europe) Day (8th)

June   Demobilisation began (18th)
                William Joyce put on trial for treason, found guilty and
                    was later hanged
                Churchill, Stalin and Truman sign the Potsdam
                    Agreement (5th)

July   The Labour Party won the General Election with a landslide
                    victory; Clement Atlee became Prime Minister (26th)

August   VJ (Victory in Japan) Day (15)
                By the end of the war some 100,000 British women had
                    married Allied servicemen; 80% married GIs

December   The divorce rate for 1945 was 25,000 compared with
                    8,000 in 1939
                The number of illegitimate births rose from 26,500 in 1940
                    to 64,000 in 1945

BIBLIOGRAPHY

The War in East Sussex, Sussex Express and County Herald, 1945
The Blitz Then and Now, Vols 1-3, ed Winston Ramsey, Battle of Britain
  Prints International
The Battle of Britain Then and Now, ed Winston Ramsey, Battle of Britain
  Prints International
The JG26 War Diary, Vol 1, Donald Caldwell, Battle of Britain Prints
The Spirit of War, Orbis Publishing, 1995
Women in Wartime, Jane Waller and Michael Vaughan-Rees, McDonald

Research was also carried out at:
The Public Record Office, Kew, London
East Sussex County Record Office, Lewes
Brighton Reference Library

German prisoners-of-war disembark at East Quay, Newhaven,
indicating that the end of the war was near.

ABOUT THE AUTHOR

David Rowland was four when war broke out on September 3, 1939. He still has vivid memories of the nights when Brighton burned, of sleeping in a Morrison shelter, of carrying a gas mask everywhere and of the many evacuations from the classroom to the air raid shelters outside Finsbury Road Junior School.

David Rowland

David's mother, Louise, died less than three weeks after he was born, and he was adopted by his aunt, Edith and her husband, Charles. Edith died on September 3, 1939, at 7am, just four hours before the outbreak of war. David then went to live with his adoptive father and his grandmother in Grove Street.

He worked at Sainsbury's before and after two years' National Service with the RAF, and in 1958 joined Brighton Borough Police, where his service included periods as a beat constable, dog handler, patrol car driver, radio and teleprinter operator and, finally, as a full time Police Federation official. He retired on medical grounds in 1985. He rejoined Sainsbury's at the Newhaven branch in 1997. His hobbies include local history, travel and the American West.

David Rowland would be pleased to hear from any readers who have information about the flying bomb incident when fifteen houses were damaged at Burrow Head, Newhaven, on Saturday, July 30, 1944. He would also be interested in information about other wartime incidents in Sussex. He may be contacted through S.B. Publications, 19 Grove Road, Seaford, Sussex BN25 1TP.